EXPERIENCING GOD'S LOVE

Five images of transformation

STEVEN CROFT

CHURCH HOUSE
PUBLISHING

Church House Publishing
Church House
Great Smith Street
London SW1P 3AZ

Published 2011 by Church House Publishing

British Library Cataloguing in Publication data

A catalogue record for this book is available from the British Library

978 07151 4251 6

Cover design by Leigh Hurlock
Inside design by Hugh Hillyard-Parker, Edinburgh
Printed and bound in Great Britain by Halstan

CONTENTS

INTRODUCTION

On my birthday in May last year I stood at the top of Niagara Falls watching as the waters poured over the edge of the Horseshoe Falls. The mists rose from the spray hundreds of feet below. Thousands of people had come to see one of the natural wonders of the world. I watched as they made their way around the tourist attractions or simply stood and gazed at the natural majesty of rock and water.

I don't know what was in their minds but I knew what I was thinking. This was only my second trip to Canada. The visit to Niagara was a day of sightseeing sandwiched between speaking engagements in Edmonton and Toronto. Thirty-five years ago I had stood in this exact spot, watching the waterfall. Then I was 20 and at the beginning of a road trip around North America with four friends. I was on the threshold of adult life: single (but about to become engaged); unclear about my life's direction (but sensing a call to ordination); unclear what might lie ahead (but looking forward to it).

It was a good moment to pause and reflect on the passage of those years: all that had happened and all the journeys that had led me back to this point. I was the same but different. Married for many years; a father of four; ordained; in mid-life; looking back as well as ahead to the rest of the journey; thankful and hopeful. These familiar words passed through my mind:

> Give thanks to the LORD for he is good;
> For his mercy endures for ever.
>
> *Psalm 107.1*

Through all of the years since I stood at the Falls, the waters have poured over the ledge at Niagara and thundered into the basin below. Through all of the years since I last visited this place, God's love has been constant, secure, vast and strong. There have been times when I've caught fresh glimpses of that love; times when I grow in my understanding; times when God's love is out of sight for a time, obscured by the mist.

This short book is a reflection on experiencing God's love as deep and strong as a waterfall. It is a follow on to *Exploring God's Mercy* (Church House Publishing, 2010). *Exploring God's Mercy* looks at five different images found in Psalm 107.

These are all images of the differences God's love and mercy make when we discover that love for the first time in and through Jesus Christ. Those who are lost find their way. The trapped are set free. The sickness in our souls finds healing. Those overwhelmed by chaos and storms find a safe harbour. The barren life bears fruit again.

Experiencing God's Love looks at five different pictures of what it means to live the Christian life. Again all the pictures are found in the psalms, although I have drawn on five different psalms for this book. These five pictures are about beginning the Christian journey, and continuing it through the whole of your life from the time at which you discover God's grace in Jesus Christ until the moment of death. The whole of the journey of faith is about God's mercy and love in Jesus Christ. The beginning of the journey is about contrasts. As we move on in the journey, experiencing God's love is about our ongoing habits and experiences growing deeper with the years.

Experiencing God's Love is written with two groups of people in mind. The first are those who have recently come to Christian faith as young people and adults. You may have taken part in a short introductory course such as an Alpha Course or the Emmaus Nurture Course. *Experiencing God's Love* aims to build on that beginning and to equip you with some of the resources and the habits you need for the journey ahead.

The second group are those who have been Christians for many years and who use the material as part of a Lent group or a regular home group, or as part of their individual reading to deepen their walk with God in the years ahead. You may not be able to remember a time when you were not a Christian. The beginning of your Christian life may be many years in the past, but it is still important and helpful to look in fresh ways, through new images at the way in which your life with God is unfolding and at ways of experiencing God's love today.

As with *Exploring God's Mercy*, each session is divided into three parts.

Experiencing God's love through the psalms

The psalms are among the oldest and most profound poems in the history of the world. For thousands of years Christians have learned them by heart. The psalms offer the whole range of emotional responses to every kind of life situation. Most of the psalms were composed for use in public worship in ancient Israel. These prayers and songs were used generation after generation, chewed over and reflected on, collected together and distilled into the book we have today. The Book of Psalms was the prayer book of Jesus and the early Church. Its images are taken up by the New Testament writers and by those who have shaped the teaching and worship of the church in every generation. The Book of Psalms is a handbook for exploring God's love.

The psalms are therefore a precious resource for Christian faith and life. However, they are little known today and there are 150 psalms in the book. Where do we begin to get to find our way around such a vast resource? In *Experiencing God's Love* we will take just five psalms, one each week, as our starting point. One of the things you may want to do is try to learn each psalm by heart as you go through the book. If you do this you will begin to build a precious resource for your own prayers and reflection for years to come. I have used my own translation of the psalm at the beginning and end of sessions but, if you are learning the psalm by heart, you may want to learn the New Revised Standard Version (which is used everywhere else in the book).

The five psalms and images we will begin to explore are:

- **Psalm 1** stands as a heading and introduction to the entire Book of Psalms. The psalm introduces the image of the Christian being rooted in God through meditation on the Scriptures. This call to be **rooted** throughout our life represents a daily choice and discipline.

- **Psalm 51** is a profound song of repentance for sin. The psalm helps us deal with the reality that even though we may know God in Christ, we also know times when we fall and fail badly. Psalm 51 introduces the image of the Christian being **washed** and cleansed by God, not only at the beginning of the journey but as we seek to grow in holiness throughout our lives.

- **Psalm 27** is a song that balances faith and anxiety. We place our trust in God in the midst of many dangers and difficulties. The psalm begins with the image of God as our **light**: in Christ we no longer live in darkness but share in the light and love of Christ.

- **Psalm 23** is still the best known of all the psalms. It is a song of faith, of quiet prayer and confidence. The psalm begins with the image of God as our shepherd: all our days we are **tended** and loved by God and experience his grace.

- Finally **Psalm 16** is a personal song of thanksgiving and celebrates God's faithfulness and ours. The psalm introduces the image of God as our host who **welcomes** us to his table both in this life and in the life to come.

As we read and explore these five psalms together and learn them by heart, we will discover and rediscover that as we live the Christian life we are rooted, washed, enlightened, tended and welcomed in the grace and love of God.

Experiencing God's love through the Gospel of John

The second part of each study follows the image from the psalms through one of the stories or sections of the Gospel of John. John's Gospel is different from the Gospels of Matthew, Mark and Luke. John leaves out some of the familiar material and chooses some different stories from the tradition at the heart of his narrative. John's Gospel assumes we already know Matthew, Mark or Luke. At certain points John slows the story of Jesus down and takes us deeper into the truth at the heart of the story. One of John's ways into this great truth is to select some of the great images of God's grace and love in Jesus Christ and to invite us to reflect upon them. Sometimes we are invited to reflect through a story of something Jesus did. Sometimes we are asked to reflect through a picture Jesus paints in words – and sometimes through both.

In each of the sessions, therefore, we will look again through a short story or imaginative reading at the way in which each of these images is used in the Gospel of John. We are reminded again that we experience God's love through being rooted in Christ the true vine, washed by Christ the healer, enlightened by Christ the light of the world; tended by Christ the good shepherd and welcomed by Christ the host at the feast.

Experiencing God's love through habits and practices

Our study and reflection should make a difference in our lives. As the final part of each session, you are invited to reflect on and try to build good habits and disciplines that will make a significant difference to the life of any Christian who practises them faithfully in both the short and long term. Some of these disciplines focus on our life and habits of prayer and worship, which build us up in different ways for our life of discipleship. Some of these disciplines focus on the care and love we show to others and the outward expression of our faith. No one will be able to follow through every single idea here. Instead focus on the one or two that seem most helpful to you at this point in your Christian life and build from here.

Prayer and reflection

Finally, each session of *Experiencing God's Love* is set in the context of prayer. On page 9 you will find a suggested order of prayer for the beginning of each session. At the end of the session I have provided an order of prayer for you to use together.

You will also find it helpful to keep some notes of the ideas that strike you as helpful both from the book and from any of the group sessions. If you are working through the sessions week by week try to find half an hour to sit down and prepare for the session by reading it to yourself and jotting down questions and ideas. The day after the session jot down any reflections you have or resolutions you make.

Experiencing God's love

We are not called to live as Christians just for a few days or a few months or in a particular season of our lives. We are not called to live as Christians in just part of our lives. We are called to be disciples of Jesus Christ in the whole of our lives. We are called to be life-long disciples – walking in fellowship with Christ and experiencing God's love year by year and season by season. We are also called to be disciples with the whole of our lives: offering our whole selves to God.

In his letter to the Romans, Paul spends the first 11 chapters of the letter exploring the grace, mercy and love of God and all that God has done for us in Christ. Reading these chapters is like standing and watching the water pour over Niagara Falls. God's grace flows in abundance. Then, at the beginning of Romans 12, Paul outlines in just a couple of verses our response to God's grace:

> I appeal to you therefore brothers and sisters, by the mercies of God, to present your bodies as a living sacrifice, holy and acceptable to God, which is your spiritual worship. Do not be conformed to this world, but be transformed by the renewing of your minds, so that you may discern what is the will of God – what is good and acceptable and perfect.
>
> *Romans 12.1–2*

Our whole lives are meant to be lived as a response to the extraordinary mercy and love of God.

Brothers and sisters, let us experience together the love and mercy of God and live in response to God's gift to us.

INTRODUCTORY NOTES FOR GROUP LEADERS

You will need a copy of this book for each member of the group. Ideally they should have the chance to read it a few weeks before you begin to study it together.

There are notes for group leaders at the beginning of each session to guide you through. It's pretty self-explanatory.

Feel free to mix and match the different elements in the session to suit your own group. The material should work well with an existing home group or one that comes together just for Lent or at some other time of the year.

You will need to be selective. Try to focus the time on the interactive parts of the session.

There are practical activities each week which require a bit of preparation and some simple equipment. These are detailed in the leader's notes.

Each session should begin with the prayers to begin the study and then move straight into the reading of the psalm.

The translation of the psalms used at the beginning and end of each session is my own translation. Elsewhere the Bible version used is the New Revised Standard Version.

Different ways to use the material

As a regular course

The themes of *Experiencing God's Love* are very well suited to those who are new to the faith and/or new to the life of the Church. The material will work very well as a regular course for those completing Alpha or Emmaus Nurture courses, or a confirmation group that chooses to stay together and go deeper.

Home groups linked to the Sunday worship

Several churches used *Exploring God's Mercy* as study material for all of their home groups or cell groups and linked the themes to their Sunday worship.

If you have ongoing home groups in your church, it can be immensely helpful to connect them all together at certain times of the year and to explore the same material. The five themes would make an excellent sermon series for the Sundays in Lent which would connect and feed into the home group studies.

In twos and threes

Not everyone is able to be part of a small group. You could work through the material in Lent with two or three friends; or as a married couple; or as an older Christian working with someone who is new to the faith. You will need to read the sessions carefully and think about them.

As a congregation

Not every church has a tradition of midweek home meetings. You could also use the materials as part of a midweek Eucharist in Lent:

● The opening prayers could be used as the preparation for the service.

● The two readings would be the Psalm section and the Gospel text (not the retelling here).

● After a short reflection the congregation could divide into groups to discuss the material and pray for one another.

● The congregation would draw together again for the Peace and for Communion.

● Parts of the closing prayers could be used at the end.

Clearly, you could not use all the material in the sessions as part of a Eucharist. Focus on the images in the psalms and leave people to read through the sections on John's Gospel and the reflections on the passion on their own.

On your own

Finally, the book is also intended to be read by individuals. If you are working through it on your own, make sure you use the times and spaces for prayer and for journaling.

God will be at work!

However you engage with the material, remember that God in his grace will be at work in you and in the other people who explore these passages. It is very powerful and life changing indeed to experience the extent of God's love for us.

OPENING PRAYERS TO BEGIN THE SESSION

If you are using this book as a group then these opening prayers should be used at the very beginning of each meeting. If you are working through this book on your own, the prayers should be used at the start of each session.

A candle is lit as a sign of God's presence and light. We say together the words in bold type. Pause between each couplet and say the words slowly and softly.

Bless the LORD, O my soul,
And all that is within me bless his holy name

Bless the LORD, O my soul,
And forget not all his benefits

Who forgives all your sins
And heals all your infirmities

Who redeems your life from the Pit
And crowns you with faithful love and compassion

Who satisfies you with good things
So that your youth is renewed like an eagle's.

Psalm 103.1–5

The group keep a time of silent thanksgiving for the signs of God's love in our lives this day.

After at least two minutes of silence, one or more people should lead in a time of thanksgiving.

A hymn or song of praise and thanksgiving can be played or sung together.

I appeal to you therefore brothers and sisters, by the mercies of God, to present your bodies as a living sacrifice, holy and acceptable to God, which is your spiritual worship. Do not be conformed to this world, but be transformed by the renewing of your minds, so that you may discern what is the will of God – what is good and acceptable and perfect.

Romans 12.1–2

This prayer is said together:

Lord Jesus Christ, we thank you
For all the benefits that you have won for us
For all the pains and insults that you have borne for us.
Most merciful redeemer, friend and brother,
May we know you more clearly,
Love you more dearly
And follow you more nearly,
Day by day. Amen.

After Richard of Chichester (1253)

After these opening prayers, move straight to the reading at the start of this week's session.

NOTES ON THE OPENING PRAYERS

Christians believe that change comes through the grace of God working within us rather than through our own efforts. As we think about transformation in these five sessions, it will be important to begin each of the five gatherings by reflecting on the grace of God and all that we are given.

The opening verses to Psalm 103 are a very helpful way to do that. One of the particular features of the psalms is that they teach us to talk to ourselves – to reflect on how we are, to offer ourselves comfort or encouragement, to see how well the strong words in the psalms 'fit' our state of mind.. Often the psalms will do that through giving us words to speak to 'my soul': the very core of our being.

Sometimes a psalm will help us to articulate a question we want to ask ourselves, as in Psalm 42.5:

> Why are you cast down, O my soul, and why are you disquieted within me?

In Psalm 103, we are encouraged to speak to our souls and encourage our inmost being to do two things. The first is to bless God and offer praise. We step away from our preoccupation with ourselves and with our own worlds and open our eyes again to see God's wonder and love and beauty. C. S. Lewis writes in his *Reflections on the Psalms* that we are called to praise God much as we are called to appreciate a great work of art or some part of the natural world. The beauty of God's grace and nature draws us into praise and wonder. Praise is a powerful medicine for the soul: we are healed from our tendency to turn inwards.

Psalm 103 also calls us to encourage our inmost being not to forget all that God has done for us. In other words, we are reminding ourselves to remember. It is not of course that we have forgotten all that God has done in the sense that we may forget someone's name if we don't see them for a long time. Rather, in the press of our daily lives, in the business of the day, in the press of our immediate activity, our awareness of all that God has done sinks lower and lower in our conscious minds.

So as we gather to think together about these pictures of transformation, it is important not to rush straight into the study. Time needs to be taken to be still, to enter into God's presence together and to call to mind all that God has done for us. These things will then be uppermost in our hearts and minds and not the cares and stresses of the day.

What are these benefits? Psalm 103 only mentions some of them. They echo some of the themes in Psalm 107. Our sins are forgiven. Our souls are being healed. Our lives are being saved from the Pit: from destruction in this life and in the life to come. We have been blessed with God's great covenant love, which is everlasting, and his compassion. When we are hungry within, God offers nourishment for our souls. When we are weary in our souls, God lifts us up.

Read the verses from Psalm 103 slowly and softly, pausing between each couplet. Too often when we worship together we belt out the words at a great pace and volume. It's better to say them slowly and let them sink in deeply. Follow the verses with a time of silence and use these moments to look back over the day and bring to mind the things you have been especially thankful for, the moments of grace, the times when you have been especially aware of God's presence.

In the spiritual exercises of St Ignatius, used and taught by the Jesuits, there is a vital exercise to be done each day called the Awareness Examen. Essentially it is a form of prayer based on thanksgiving and becoming attentive to the signs of God's presence in our lives. This requires stillness.

You may want to have a different person leading the opening prayers each week and that person will need to judge the length of silence that is most helpful but try to keep at least two minutes at this point to be still together and then invite people to lead in prayers of thanksgiving.

Many hymns and worship songs draw their inspiration from these verses in Psalm 103. If your group is musical you may like to sing one each week. The best known is Henry Lyte's hymn, 'Praise my soul the King of Heaven'. It preserves the same form of personal address to my soul, to the heart of my being with the powerful opening lines:

> Praise my soul the King of Heaven,
> To his feet thy tribute bring;
> Ransomed, healed, restored, forgiven,
> Who like me his praise should sing?

The verses of the psalm and the silence and thanksgiving set us once again in the right place before God as we begin. These are then followed by the verses from the beginning of Romans 12 which remind the group of the overall theme of the sessions. We are giving thanks for the grace and love of God in our lives. God's love has redeemed us and God's love is changing and transforming us as we journey together with him.

Our part is to co-operate with that process of transformation. For that reason we are called to offer our lives to God as a living sacrifice. This verse is echoed, of course, in the prayer which many Christian traditions use at the end of the Eucharist:

> Almighty God,
> We thank you for feeding us
> With the body and blood of your son, Jesus Christ.
> Through him we offer you our souls and bodies
> To be a living sacrifice.
> Send us in the power of your spirit
> To live and work to your praise and glory.
> Amen.

The verses from Romans summon us to the work of change and transformation. The world around us will try to shape us into its own mould. We are subject every day to all kinds of pressure to conform: in our dress, in our lifestyle, in our patterns of spending and borrowing, in our relationships. These pressures come from the media and wider culture and from our background and history. They are immensely strong forces which shape our lives and characters.

Paul's words remind us that we are called to be transformed through the renewing of our minds. The reflection we will do together is part of that process of transformation and change. That process is founded on experiencing the love of God. The transforming of our minds enables us to see much more clearly God's will for us in all of the choices and decisions of our lives.

Finally, the opening prayers introduce one of the great prayers from the English Christian tradition to be said together each week: the prayer of St Richard of Chichester. The prayer is about transformation and our daily walk of discipleship. It became well known again in the 1960s as the foundation of one of the songs in the musical *Godspell*, 'Day by Day'.

I've included the prayer for two reasons. The first is that it catches very powerfully the sense of discipleship as a daily walk with God and a daily transformation. But the second and more important reason is that the prayer roots that transformation in the work of Jesus Christ on the cross. Christ in this prayer is far more than a model or good example for us (though he does set the pattern for our lives and characters). In his death on the cross for our sins, Jesus Christ has borne our sorrows and the consequences of our sin. Through his death on the cross, Jesus Christ has won for us great benefits – the same benefits we called to mind in Psalm 103. The cross is the greatest demonstration of the love of God in Jesus Christ. It is through the cross that we know how long and high and wide and deep is the love of God in Christ. It is through the benefits of the cross that we can know God's love for ourselves.

SESSION 1

ROOTED

notes for group leaders

You will need to give some time at the beginning to explain the purpose of the studies and, if this is a new group, to enable people to introduce themselves (or talk in pairs and introduce one another).

Approximate timings for the session are:

Welcome; opening prayers and reflection	15 mins
Sharing your story	15 mins
Film or song clip	5 mins
A testimony (reading and reflection)	10 mins
Sharing together	20 mins
Habits and practices	15 mins
Final worship and prayers together	10 mins

There is a lot of material in each session so you will need to select from week to week.

Additional activities

The activity for the session is repotting plants. This will take some advance thought and preparation. You could go to a garden centre and buy enough small plants and big plantpots for everyone (together with compost). You will also need a surface covered in newspaper and some small trowels and facilities for handwashing.

Alternatively, you could ask every member of the group to bring a plant that is ready for repotting which they would repot during the session and give to someone else. That way you would only need a selection of plantpots and the compost.

There is a short sound file on the Church House Publishing website which introduces the session. If you decide to use this, it can be played after the initial reading of the psalm. To find the clip go to **www.chpublishing.co.uk/experiencinggodslove** and follow the link.

Involving the group

You may want to involve different members of the group in:

- Leading the opening and closing worship.
- Providing the plants and compost and the refreshments.
- Reading the story.

Ideas for film clips and music tracks

There are some very good clips on YouTube which show plants growing roots. Go to www.youtube.com and search for 'roots growing time lapse'.

If your group is musical, the song 'You are the vine, we are the branches' would be a good one to end the session.

For some weeks I will suggest a clip from a television makeover programme. A TV programme, 'Groundforce', ran some years ago in which each week a garden was transformed. There are DVDs available and also a few clips on YouTube.

Decisions and advance notice for next week

You will need to make a decision about whether you go for hand washing or foot washing in the session next week – it may affect what some people wear. Invite the group to research and, if they can, bring a photograph of their own baptism.

ROOTED

Begin with the opening prayers on page 9.

> Blessed is the one who does not walk in the ways of the wicked
> **Who will not stand in the paths of the sinner or sit in the mocker's chair**
>
> This one delights in the law of the LORD
> **and ponders that law by day and by night**
>
> This one will be like a tree rooted beside streams of water
> A tree which bears fruit in its season and whose leaves will not wither
> **Everything this person does will prosper**
>
> The wicked are not like this
> **They are like chaff which the wind scatters**
>
> The wicked will not stand in the judgement
> **Sinners will not stand in the congregation of the righteous**
>
> For the LORD knows the way of the righteous
> **But the way of the wicked shall perish.**
>
> *Psalm 1*

Part 1 Experiencing God's love through the psalm

How deep are your roots in the place where you live? I meet many people who have lived in the same place all their lives. Only last week I confirmed a young woman in her early twenties with her mother. Her grandmother and her great grandmother were present in the congregation and have lived in the same village all their lives. Others have moved away from the place where they grew up but move somewhere and settle, putting down deep roots in the soil of the local community and coming to see it as home. The city of Sheffield is full of people who moved here as students or in mid life and have taken root here. Other people find their life's journey takes them to many different places. They live in each for a few years only and find it hard to settle anywhere. Still others have been forced to move away from their place of choice because of life's hard circumstances and have to make a new life, sometimes on the other side of the world, but it never quite feels like home. The Lent course I led last year in Sheffield Cathedral had a small group of refugees and asylum seekers from a local church who were doing their best to settle after having to leave their country of origin.

You find out how deep your roots are when you have to move away. My wife and I lived in Halifax for nine years. Halifax is also where I was born. Two of our four children were also born there. We were part of a great church community. We had our roots deep in Yorkshire soil. When the time came to move away, it felt as though our lives were being pulled up by the roots. There were feelings of pain and loss. We also felt 'not at home' in our new home for quite some time.

Psalm 1 uses the powerful image of the roots of a tree to describe a life that is grounded and centred upon God. As you may know, the roots of a tree extend far below the earth. The roots have two main functions in the tree's life. First and foremost they act as an anchor. They keep the tree in its place in the midst of storms and high winds. A tree has to grow in a particular place and stay there. When trees are first planted, they often need a strong stake driven into the ground to given them security and stability. As they put down their roots, the stake can be taken away.

But the roots are also the way in which the tree draws in water and nutrients from the earth to feed its own life. Year by year the tree adds a ring of wood, it bears leaves and it bears fruit only because its roots are driven down deep and drawing up good things.

Trees need a lot of water to grow. In most places in Britain, they do very well. Our land is still covered by acres of forest. I am told that Sheffield has more trees than any other city in England. My grass turns brown quickly in the summer because the trees in the garden draw in the water. In the land where this psalm was written, the ground is very fertile but the climate is very dry. Good things only grow and bear fruit where there is water in abundance. A running stream coming down from the mountains is the best form of irrigation. A tree planted near its banks will put down deep roots which will extend under and around the bed of the stream, drawing up the water which the tree needs for its life. Sometimes the stream will not be visible on the surface but will flow under the earth. When all the valley around is as dry as dust and nothing grows at all, still the trees in the water bed of the stream are green and fertile. They bear their fruit in due season.

Trees take time to grow. There is nothing hasty about them, as Treebeard says in the *Lord of the Rings*. Plant one today and it will be many years until it comes to maturity. Roots are part of the very structure and fabric of the tree and they take time to grow as well, pushing down through soil and rock to find the source of life. But the roots of a tree are also immensely strong: they crack paving stones and ponds and anything else that gets in their way.

The central image of roots is of course only part of the psalm. Psalm 1 is placed at the very beginning to offer anyone who comes to this book a choice. Here is a path forking in the road. The way of the righteous leads to the right, the way of the wicked to the left. Choose one or the other. Remember all of the choices offered to us by Jesus in the Sermon on the Mount and all through Matthew's Gospel. Will it be the wide road or the narrow one? Will I be like the wise or foolish house builder? Will I choose to be a sheep or a goat? A Pharisee or a tax collector?

Our world today likes choice but not this kind of choice. We are shaped by our culture as consumers so we love the kind of choice that is both/and. We want to be able to have both a starter and a pudding. To choose one thing for us no longer means we can't have something else. It is very good for us to realize in a deeper way that some choices really are alternatives. We cannot turn to the right and to the left. We have to choose on the one hand the way of the wicked, the seat of the mocker, to stand with the scornful. Or we can choose the way of the righteous: the Way of the Lord.

This choice, like many others, has consequences in our lives. It shapes the people we become over the whole course of our years. If we choose the way of the wicked, the psalmists tell us, then our lives will become light and inconsequential and much less than they would otherwise be. We will be like the husks of corn, easily blown away by the wind. If we choose the Way of the Lord then this is a call to put down deep roots, slowly and steadily over time, to grow in our stability and our sense of being anchored to the good soil and able in every season of our lives to grow fruit.

So the psalm is about choice. The text invites us to consider what kind of people we want to become. Will we choose to become people of weight and maturity, anchored and rooted, living lives of purpose and bearing fruit?

Will we seek to leave our mark on the world and a legacy wherever we go? Or will we choose live lives that are as light and inconsequential as chaff which the wind scatters in a moment?

We don't need to do anything to choose the second of these options. It is the default option and the course our lives will take as we drift with the crowd. Many people never even notice that their lives are becoming less significant and less than they could be. In the words of Romans 12, you don't need to do anything to make sure your life is conformed or shaped by this world. That will happen all by itself. Sometimes we see it happening in ourselves or other people but most of the time the default way to live is to sit back and blend in. Our lives are much less than they could be because it is easier to flow with the tide than to resist it.

So what does it mean to choose the different path? The psalm is very clear that this different path would not be open to us at all without God's grace and call. It simply would not be there if God had not provided a way. We would not know God's love if God had not revealed his love to us in the Scriptures and also in his Son Jesus Christ. We would not be able to grow in our knowledge of his love and in the depth of our lives if God had not provided the very ways we grow and develop: the means of grace.

Growth in depth and becoming rooted is then a work of grace. It is more God's work than ours. If God did not set in our hearts a hunger to know him and a longing to be rooted and to bear fruit, then we could not pursue this pathway. But, as the psalm implies, there is still a choice to be made. There is still a calling to respond to God's grace offered to us. There is still a challenge to accept the call to grow in depth and stability in the ways God has provided.

The choice we need to make is not in this case a one-off decision (like the decision to be married or to become a Christian). This choice is to form and be formed in a particular habit and way of life. That habit and way of life is to choose to delight in and to ponder the law of the Lord, the word of God.

What is this law and why is it so important? The Hebrew word for law is Torah. The Torah for the Hebrews (and for the Jews today) are the five Books of Moses, the first five books of the Christian Old Testament. By extension, the term comes to mean the whole of the Scriptures and for the Christian that means both the Old and the New Testament. The Word of God in Scripture is a gift, a grace from God. But it is a gift that needs to be received, explored, delighted in and pondered. The habit of engaging with God's word is meant to be a daily habit if we are to live lives that make a difference, that are rooted and that bear fruit in due season. Psalm 119 is another much longer psalm which explores the wonder of God's Torah through a whole range of images.

The Scriptures are an amazing treasure, a source of life, a world to be explored, daily bread for the soul.

For the Christian, though, there is still more to discovering God's love through the Word of God. Christians believe that we cannot work out for ourselves who God is. When human beings try to do that we fall into all kinds of errors and over and over again we end up creating gods in our own image. This is idolatry. Christians believe that God in his grace and love has revealed himself to us in two ways. The first way is through the Scriptures: through God's word spoken and written down for God's people in every generation. The second way is through God's own Son being born as a human child and living among us and revealing to us what God is like. In the opening words of the letter to the Hebrews:

> Long ago God spoke to our ancestors in many and various ways by the prophets but in these last days he has spoken to us by a Son, whom he appointed heir of all things, through whom he also created the worlds.
>
> *Hebrews 1.1*

Long ago the Old Testament prophets realized that God's word was not like human speech. God's word has power to create, to bring about that which it describes, to bear fruit in different ways, to challenge and rebuke. In the story of creation at the beginning of Genesis, when God speaks the whole universe is created and flows from his word.

For Christians these two ways in which God reveals himself are not in contrast. They are two parts of the same whole. For that reason, at the very beginning of John's Gospel, Jesus is introduced first as God's Word, taking human form, in words that echo the first chapter of Genesis:

> In the beginning was the Word and the Word was with God and the Word was God. He was in the beginning with God.
>
> *John 1.1−2*

> And the Word become flesh and lived among us and we have seen his glory, the glory as of a father's only son, full of grace and truth.
>
> *John 1.14*

When Christians reflect on the choice and the challenge of Psalm 1 to delight in God's law and ponder it day and night, we mean the whole of God's revelation of himself in the written word and in the Living Word, Jesus Christ.

Meditation and reflection on Scripture and on the character and person of Jesus is at the heart of learning to be transformed in the renewing of our minds.

At the heart of this session then is God's gift to us of a stream of living water flowing deep beneath the surface of our lives. God's call to us is the call to put down deep roots through being formed in a daily habit of prayer and engaging with the Scriptures. It is only in this way that we will be able to live lives that are distinctive and that bear fruit in due season.

Sharing your story

Take a little while to introduce yourself to the person sitting next to you or to the whole group in terms of your roots. Where did you come from originally? Where have you felt most at home in your life? Where do you feel most settled? What helps you put down roots in the place where you live?

Think of some people who seem to you to be rooted and to be people of weight and substance. What do you think lies beneath the surface of their lives to help them be that kind of person? Think of people who seem light and insubstantial. What do you learn?

Is it difficult to be a Christian? Are we trying to grow in a dry and thirsty land?

Now think together about what it means for a Christian to be rooted in God. Many Christians have never developed a habit of regular personal prayer and exploring the Scriptures. What is attractive about such a habit? What help and strength would it give?

You may want to share as a whole group; or one person might prepare in advance and tell part of their story; or you might want to share in twos or threes.

If you are reading this book on your own then take some time at this point to journal and look back on the way this sense of being rooted has surfaced in your life.

A film or song clip

See page 16 for suggestions.

Part 2 Experiencing God's love through the Gospel of John

A testimony

One of the group should read the story aloud.

Yes, I remember the wedding. None of us forgot that day. It's a story I've told many times. We'd been invited at the last minute. The couple were friends of Jesus' family from Nazareth days. A few of us were staying in a nearby town overnight. We never stayed very long in one place even then.

One of the things I loved first about Jesus was the unexpected things he did. You never quite knew what was going to happen next. My life had been very predictable before I met him. I got up. I went to work. I came home. I did my chores. I went to synagogue. With Jesus every day was different. Every time we thought we knew what he was going to do, something different happened.

The night before the wedding, we were sitting round chatting after the meal: just friends getting to know each other still. 'Master,' I asked him, 'why does every day with you seem different from the day before?' 'Come and see tomorrow,' he said. 'I'll wake you.'

We went to bed late and the next day I felt his hand on my shoulder an hour before dawn. I tumbled out of bed and dressed. Jesus was heading out of the door already. He'd woken a couple of the others as well. We followed him as we so often did. He led us out of the house, out of the town and up into the hills to a deserted place. And there he stood or sat or knelt for a while in silence for what seemed a very long time. We watched from a distance.

After about an hour he came back to join us. He looked at me. 'Now do you understand?' 'Not really,' I said. 'You will later,' he replied. 'Now – the wedding.'

Things were well underway when we arrived in Cana. The whole village was at the wedding. The bride looked great. The bridegroom looked worried. The children played under the tables. The older women gossiped in one corner. The men talked business to one another. Everyone wore their best clothes.

As soon as we arrived, Mary came up to Jesus in relief. 'They've run out of wine,' she said. That's a serious thing at a wedding. Even I could see now that something was wrong. There were angry conversations taking place behind the table. The bridegroom's new mother-in-law had a thundercloud over her head.

As I remember it now, Jesus paused for a moment as though he was checking out something deep inside. He smiled at his mother. Mary was another of those people who were always doing the unexpected. 'Woman what concern is that to you and me? My hour is not yet come.' It sounds a bit harsh now when the story is told, but you had to hear the affection in his voice and see the smile in his eyes.

Mary smiled back and she called over the servants. She gathered them round. We were crowding in to listen, of course. She gave them their instructions. I've never forgotten them: 'Do whatever he tells you.'

The rest of the story is well known of course. There were six stone water jars each holding twenty gallons. Jesus never did things by halves. Jesus told them to fill the jars with water. There was lots of grumbling. It took about an hour. The wedding feast went on the whole time of course and every now and again you could see a the panic about the wine beginning to spread. The guests were very polite but you could tell the story of the wedding without wine would be told in Cana for generations.

When the last jar was filled to the brim Jesus said to the servants: 'Now draw some water out and take it to the chief steward.' They looked at Jesus as if he was mad. Then they looked at Mary and she nodded. The servants shrugged their shoulders and did as they were asked.

The chief steward was having a bad day. His job was on the line. He looked relieved and curious and worried all at the same time until he tasted what was in the cup. Then he looked as though he couldn't believe his eyes. He downed the goblet in one gulp and held out the empty cup for more. From the other side of the room we could see him asking where the wine came from and how much there was. The servants motioned to the six jars brimming to the top with the best wine. We could smell it now. The chief steward's legs gave way. He had to sit down.

The servants started to give out the wine. The whole atmosphere at the wedding changed. The party went on all night. I'm afraid I don't remember much from that point on – except the words of the chief steward to the bridegroom:

'Everyone serves the good wine first and then the inferior wine after the guests have become drunk. But you have kept the good wine until now.'

Jesus came to find us sleeping in the corner early the next morning while it was still dark. 'Wake up,' he said. 'Come and see.'

Once again we followed him at a distance out of the house, out of the town, up into the hills. He stood and sat and knelt and prayed. Another unexpected day was about to begin.

Retold from John 2.1–10

'I am the vine, you are the branches. Those who abide in me and I in them bear much fruit, because apart from me you can do nothing.'

John 15.5

Sharing together

Share together in the work of planting and repotting. Take a good look at the root structure of the different plants.

As you share the work together, take it in turns to share the ways in which you have looked to sink down roots into the earth as a tree.

If you like, you may want to use the very similar image from John 15 of the branch abiding (and being rooted securely) in the stem of the vine. John's Gospel describes Jesus' miracles as signs. The wedding at Cana which produces wine (made from grapes) is the first of the signs. The Gospel also has a series of sayings in which Jesus describes himself as 'I am...' The last of these is, 'I am the vine.' The whole central part of the gospel is framed by this image of being rooted and bearing fruit.

Who is helping you to grow these roots?

Remember to keep the emphasis in your conversation on God's grace in providing these ways to grow more deeply into his love. Growth is about discovering and deepening that sense of grace.

Part 3 Experiencing God's love through habits and practices

Here is a series of habits and practices to work on in the coming year to help you feel rooted. I suggest you choose just two and reflect on them with a couple of friends as you go through the year. Each is about growing deeper roots. You may like to picture your life as like a tree and be honest about the depth of your roots in Christ. How might you look to extend and grow them?

Public worship and the Eucharist

Many Christians are losing their common discipline of Sunday worship with God's people. Other things crowd into the week. Many new Christians struggle to establish this. Can you commit yourself this year to public worship at the same time every week without having to think twice about it? Or if you work on Sundays is there another midweek service or Sunday evening service that can provide your staple diet on those Sundays. Our public worship is a sign of the response to God's grace in the whole of our lives.

Private prayer and Bible reading

Surprisingly few Christians ever develop strong habits of private prayer and Bible reading. Yet this was so clearly part of the life of Jesus and a pattern he commends to his disciples. Choosing to make this time is one of the most critical choices we can make in terms of being formed into the likeness of Christ and not conformed to this world.

Different people have different rhythms of life and work. But for most of us the early morning will be the best. There are many different ways to pray and explore Scripture. You may want to talk with other members of the group about what is and isn't helpful. You are not aiming to cover everything by Easter but lay a foundation for the habits of a lifetime.

Quiet days and retreat

Many Christians find they benefit enormously from a regular time away at a Christian festival or retreat centre or place of pilgrimage. Such times insert a moment to pause in our lives. We stop and think and reflect and gain perspective on where we are travelling and any course corrections we need to make. Many local churches build this kind of day into their calendar. If it's not there in your own church perhaps your group could arrange something for other people to join in. Other people find it helpful to go away by themselves to a religious community or retreat house for a few days and take time to grow a deeper walk with God.

Companions on the journey

Talking about our prayer life can be quite difficult as the ideas and thoughts that come to us in prayer are deeply personal. For that reason a confidential relationship in which we share something of what is going on with someone who is more experienced in prayer and the Way can be very helpful indeed. This may be very informal and happen through fellowship and pastoral care in the local church. However, there are times when it can be helpful to have a more formal relationship with a spiritual director or soul friend, often outside your own congregation. Ask if other members of your group have any experience of this and how you would go about finding someone in your own context.

For discussion

● Which of these habits and practices will you pay attention to in the coming year?
● What new insights about God's love are you taking away from this session?

Prayers together

Before you pray, spend a few moments in quietness and rest and look at the plants you have repotted or the seeds you have planted.

Blessed is the one who does not walk in the ways of the wicked
Who will not stand in the paths of the sinner or sit in the mocker's chair

This one delights in the law of the LORD
and ponders that law by day and by night

This one will be like a tree rooted beside streams of water
A tree which bears fruit in its season and whose leaves will not wither
Everything this one does will prosper

The wicked are not like this
They are like chaff which the wind scatters

The wicked will not stand in the judgement
Sinners will not stand in the congregation of the righteous

For the LORD knows the way of the righteous
But the way of the wicked shall perish.

Psalm 1

A time of open prayer or one person may lead prepared intercessions.

Pray for one another and for any questions that have arisen.

Pray for one another in your intention to grow deeper roots.

End with the Lord's Prayer introduced by:

Trusting in the compassion of God,
As our Saviour taught us so we pray:
Our Father in heaven ...

Now, LORD, you let your servant go in peace;
Your word has been fulfilled.

My own eyes have seen the salvation
Which you have prepared in the sight of every people.

A light to reveal you to the nations
And the glory of your people Israel.

Glory to the Father and to the Son
And to the Holy Spirit
As it was in the beginning, is now
And shall be for ever. Amen.

The Song of Simeon

Bless the LORD, O my soul,
And all that is within me bless his holy name

Bless the LORD, O my soul,
And forget not all his benefits

Who forgives all your sins
And heals all your infirmities

Who redeems your life from the Pit
And crowns you with faithful love and compassion

Who satisfies you with good things
So that your youth is renewed like an eagle's.

Psalm 103.1–5

For reflection and practice by group members after the session

● Write down the steps you need to take to grow deeper roots in the ways you discussed in the session.

● Take one practical step in this direction.

WASHED

notes for group leaders

Approximate timings for the session are:

Welcome; opening prayers and reflection	15 mins
Sharing your story	15 mins
Film or song clip	5 mins
A testimony (reading and reflection)	10 mins
Sharing together	20 mins
Habits and practices	15 mins
Final worship and prayers together	10 mins

There is a lot of material in each session so you will need to select from week to week.

Additional activities

The activity for the session is foot or hand washing. I suggest you take a little time to agree with the group whether you wash feet or hands or a mixture.

You will need towels and a basin and if possible a large jug of warm water to pour into the basin at the beginning. You may also want to think about playing a Christian song or some music during the exercise.

There is a short sound file on the Church House Publishing website which introduces the session. If you decide to use this, it can be played after the initial reading of the psalm. To find the clip go to **www.chpublishing.co.uk/experiencinggodslove** and follow the link.

Involving the group

You may want to involve different members of the group in:

- Leading the opening and closing worship.

- Providing the equipment for the washing and the refreshments.

- Reading the story.

Ideas for film clips and music tracks

The classic TV makeover programme on the theme of being washed is 'How clean is your house'? The Channel 4 website has some clips and trailers for the programme which show classically dirty kitchens and other areas that would introduce another dimension to the session.

The songs 'The Servant King' and 'Brother, Sister, let me serve you' would be ideal for the session.

People will have been asked to bring photographs of their baptism and to share them. You may also want to research a copy of Rembrandt's famous painting, 'The Return of the Prodigal Son', to illustrate one of the points made in the text.

Advance notice for next week

The activity next week is lighting candles together. You might want to ask members of the group to bring any candles they have to help with the session.

SESSION 2

WASHED

Begin with the opening prayers on page 9.

Have mercy on me, O God, according to your steadfast love
According to your great gentleness, wipe away my sins

Wash me through and through from my iniquity
And from all my sins please make me clean

For I know my transgressions all too well
My sin is before my eyes continually

Against you and you alone I have sinned
I have done great evil in your sight

Therefore you are right to pass sentence on me
And accurate in your judgement

Truly I was conceived in iniquity
In sin did my mother conceive me

Truly it is truth you long for deep within
So in my secret heart please teach me wisdom

Purge me with hyssop and I shall be clean
Wash me and I shall be whiter than snow

Let me hear joy and celebration again
Let the bones you have crushed rejoice

Turn away your face from my sins
Hide all of my iniquities

A clean heart create in me, O God,
An upright spirit set deep within me.

Psalm 51.1–10

Part 1 Experiencing God's love through the psalm

Think back to your most vivid memory of what it means to be dirty. You may want to go back to your childhood or perhaps to a camping or walking holiday. It may not be a pleasant experience. I used to play rugby as a school boy (badly). I'm very short sighted so I would always be picked as part of the scrum. The game used to consist of falling over in the mud, picking myself up again, looking for the largest concentration of players and running towards it, pushing in the right direction and falling over in the mud again.

When I was a young man, I spent some time working as an assistant gardener for the parks department. One rainy day my day's work was to collect an enormous pile of horse manure from a farmyard and load it onto a little truck in several loads and take it back to the park for use on the rose beds. It was a very windy day and I was shovelling into the wind. By the end of the day I was absolutely covered in the stuff. I can still remember travelling home on the crowded bus and the way people tried to avoid me.

When you've got your memory of being dirty fixed in your mind, then picture what it feels like to sink into a hot bath or a shower or a hot tub. There is something about hot water and soap that not only cleanses us but revives us as well. The grime and dust of the day fall away. We emerge a new person. For many who work outdoors or in factories or mines or on the farm, this experience is a daily one.

Psalm 51 takes this everyday experience of being dirty and made clean and uses that experience to help us think about our relationship with God. The psalm is one long song of confession. The traditional heading for the psalm gives it a setting in the life of David at the very moment when he had committed one of the worst public sins of his life: adultery with Bathsheba and the murder of her husband, Uriah the Hittite. The sin was a massive abuse of the power of the king and the trust David had been given. It is told in 2 Samuel 11 and 12 and is a minor masterpiece of storytelling.

Psalm 51 would be available as a song or prayer in the temple for personal use and in times when a public figure such as the king needed to make a solemn act of penitence seeking God's favour for the nation. The final verses of the psalm date from the time of the exile in Babylon and speak of God rebuilding the walls of Jerusalem. In those years at least the psalm was used as a public lament and acknowledgement of the sin of the whole community. Sacrifice of animals and grain could not be offered because the temple had been destroyed. The nation found comfort in the truth that a different kind of sacrifice acceptable to God was a broken spirit and a contrite heart (51.17).

At the heart of the psalm are the prayers to be made clean:

> **Wash me through and through from my iniquity**
> **And from all my sins please make me clean.**
>
> *Psalm 51.2*

> **Purge me with hyssop and I shall be clean**
> **Wash me and I shall be whiter than snow.**
>
> *Psalm 51.7*

The psalm is not of course talking about outward cleanliness but an inner washing and cleansing of the soul. The image is one of the sins we commit staining our lives. Every wrong action and word and thought leaves its residue. These build up over time. There is nothing we can do by ourselves to clean up the mess and wipe away their effects. We throw ourselves on God's love and mercy. We seek his forgiveness and a great washing.

This sense of feeling dirty and being unclean is a universal human experience. Everyone knows what guilt feels like as a stain on the soul. Over time, to be sure, people's consciences become hardened and they suppress the sense of needing to be cleansed. But from time to time in every life there are moments of clarity and honesty when people catch a glimpse of themselves in the true mirror and become aware of how much they need to be made clean.

Experiencing God's love is not of course about realizing how dirty and stained your life is. Experiencing God's love is about the experience of being washed, forgiven and made clean. We cannot earn that forgiveness. Our souls can be washed and our sins forgiven only through faith in Jesus Christ and in his death on the cross.

On the night before Jesus died, at supper with his friends, he took a cup of wine, gave thanks and gave it to his disciples saying:

> **'... this is my blood of the covenant, which is poured out for**
> **many for the forgiveness of sins.'**
>
> *Matthew 26.27*

There are so many different ways to understand the death of Jesus on the cross and so many layers of meaning. However, right at the centre of those meanings is the simple truth that Jesus gave his life on the cross so that our sins can be forgiven – so that my sins can be forgiven – and so that I can be reconciled to

God. In the blood of Jesus shed on the cross, there is complete cleansing and a washing away of the dirt and stains of sin.

Long before the time of Christ, the prophet Isaiah foretells a time when sins will be forgiven and uses the homely image of laundry and of stains being removed:

> Come now let us argue it out, says the LORD; though your sins are like scarlet, they shall be like snow; though they are red like crimson, they shall become like wool.

Isaiah 1.18

In the Book of Revelation, John has a powerful vision of heaven: a great multitude of people clothed in white and singing praise to God. He asks one of the elders who they are. The elder replies:

> 'These are they who have come out of the great ordeal; they have washed their robes and made them white in the blood of the lamb.'

Revelation 7.14

If you have grown up in the Christian faith or if you have been a Christian for many years, it is very easy indeed to take this offer of washing and cleansing and forgiveness of sin for granted or as an automatic right. A picture grows in our minds that God is like an indulgent parent who turns a blind eye to our transgressions and forgets about them. That is not the picture offered in Scripture at all. Our wrong doing is serious. It stains and corrupts our souls and harms others deeply. God does not forget or overlook our transgressions. God forgives them. And God forgives them only because of the sacrifice of Jesus on the cross.

The sacrament of baptism is, of course, the outward and visible sign of this inward and invisible washing away of our sins. The baptism service begins with these words:

> 'Here we are washed by the Holy Spirit and made clean.'

Later the priest prays over the water:

> 'Now sanctify this water that by the power of your Holy Spirit they may be cleansed from sin and born again.'

Baptism is a sign of the complete washing, rebirth and new beginning when a person comes to faith in Christ for the first time. No matter how long we have been a Christian, it is important to remember and give thanks and rediscover

God's love in this great washing of our souls. In many churches, we walk past the font or baptistery on the way into the church as a visible reminder that we have been washed or made clean. There may also be a stoup of holy water from the font so that those coming to worship can sign themselves with the cross as a reminder that we have been made clean. One of the best ways to remember the special gift of forgiveness and washing is to walk the journey again with a person who has recently become a Christian, perhaps as they prepare for baptism and confirmation, and to see the faith again through their eyes.

However, Psalm 51 remains an important prayer in the Christian life because for all of us the experience of dirt and sin does not go away. There may be only one great washing of baptism but there are countless little washings along the way as we experience God's grace. Each time we come to worship and confess our sins we are praying for God's forgiveness and cleansing. Each time we fall away from the Christian faith outwardly or inwardly we need God's cleansing and forgiveness. One of the things we should pray for in Lent is a deeper self-awareness to see the areas of our lives now that need to be washed.

In Rembrandt's wonderful painting of the return of the prodigal son, it is very easy indeed to see that the younger son needs to be washed. The back of his head and neck, his hands, his legs and his feet are caked in dirt. He has been on the road for many months. His clothes are ragged and torn. His sandals are broken. As we look at the picture, he is clearly the one who needs to be washed.

But then our eyes pull back and we see the elder brother as Rembrandt has painted him, watching the prodigal's return and already judging both his younger brother and his own father. The dirt is not visible on the surface of his life but is very clear to those who hear Jesus' story. There is real grace in the truth that no matter how long we have been Christians, no matter what we have done, there is grace and forgiveness and washing for all who come to seek it.

> 'And this is what some of you used to be. But you were washed,
> you were sanctified, you were justified in the name of the LORD
> Jesus Christ and in the Spirit of our God.'

We experience God's love in the great washing when we first come to Christ. We confess our sins and place our trust in Christ and we are made clean by his love and mercy. There is nothing we can do to earn that forgiveness on our own or make ourselves clean. God's grace cannot be earned it must be received.

Yet each of us knows clearly that we go on sinning. We are not made holy in an instant. The journey towards holiness is long and difficult. Some of our sin is deeply ingrained within us. We have to deal with much from the past that needs changing or healing in our hearts and characters. God's continual washing away of our sins is a profound gift. We give in to new temptations and commit new sins as we grow older. Young people might struggle with lust or ambition. Older people give in more easily to bitterness, jealousy or greed. God's continual washing of our souls remains a precious grace. As we grow more mature in years and in our faith, hopefully we see ourselves more clearly. Sometimes that self-knowledge is painfully gained. We see ourselves reflected back in our mistakes and difficulties as well as the things that have gone well.

Try to imagine if you can, the Christian faith without the grace of being washed and forgiven. It is impossible. No family or friendship can survive for very long without the capacity to forgive and be forgiven. No Christian journey can last long without it either.

The further we travel in the Christian Way, the more clearly we should know that we stand in need of God's washing, cleansing and forgiveness in each twist and turn of the journey. This experience of being washed and knowing ourselves forgiven is one of the deepest experiences of God's love.

Sharing your story

Share with one another the story of your own baptism using the pictures you have brought along.

Think back to a time when you were really dirty physically. What did it feel like to step into the bath or the shower?

Talk a little if you can about your recent experience of being washed in God's love. What do the prayers of confession mean to you when you come to church? What kind of prayers of confession do you use in your own prayer?

Where do you feel you are making progress in growing more like Christ? Where do you need help and support?

You may want to share as a whole group; or one person might prepare in advance and tell part of their story; or you might want to share in twos or threes.

If you are reading this book on your own then take some time at this point to journal and look back on the way this sense of being washed has surfaced in your life.

A film or song clip

See page 32 for suggestions.

Part 2 Experiencing God's love through the Gospel of John

A testimony

Two people in the group should read the story aloud, each speaking alternate lines.

This is one of those stories about Jesus that everyone sort of knows.

But not everyone understands the reasons.

It had been a long hot day. We were staying in Jerusalem. It was Passover.

Most of the time we got on pretty well as a group – but not that week. There was tension everywhere in the city. We knew we were in danger.

Things were coming to a head. The air almost crackled. No one liked it.

Tempers frayed in the group. The hot weather didn't help. We had our work cut out whenever Jesus walked through the city. Some of the crowds tried to get rough. They asked us questions all day long.

There was no peace. We felt like strangers in the city: roughnecks from Galilee. All day long we were pushed and jostled.

We'd all started to argue as well. There was lots of jockeying for position. If things were coming to a head, everyone wanted to make sure of their own place – to sit nearest to Jesus, to be the most important.

When we made it to that upper room, we were exhausted, ready to flop down and eat whatever was there.

There was food and drink but it wasn't well prepared. We were hungry. We couldn't be bothered even to give thanks. The day had gone really badly.

One or two were showing off and trying to impress Jesus. I just sat in the corner, too tired to move. The dust was everywhere. I felt dirty somehow.

I just wanted to go home – away from the noise and the crowds and the dirt. Following Jesus was much harder than I'd ever realized.

We lay on the benches to eat with our legs facing outwards and the food in the middle. Everyone was talking in twos and threes round the table. There were little quarrels all around the room.

Some were just plain rude to each other. Some were teasing but there was a real edge to it that night. Some were openly quarrelling.

There was no fanfare. It took a few minutes to work out what was happening.

Jesus got up from the table. He took off his outer robe.

I just thought the room was a bit warm.

Then he picked up a towel. I broke off the conversation with the man next to me. Then he poured some water into a basin.

He was standing where everyone could see him. It was quite a big basin – he poured two or three buckets of water out of those big stone jars. Every conversation stopped and all eyes turned to him.

Then Jesus took his basin and his towel and he knelt at the feet of the man next to him. Like all of us, he'd just kicked off his sandals when he lay down to eat.

Jesus poured water over his feet and with his own hands he washed them with soap till they were clean. With his own hands. He poured water again and rinsed them. Then he dried them.

He didn't say a word. He just looked deep into that man's eyes. The man looked away ashamed at first. Then he looked back right into Jesus' eyes.

Something began to change in the room. The atmosphere started to lift. Peter didn't get it.

Peter never got it. He protested: 'Lord are you going to wash my feet?'

Jesus answered him patiently. He was very tired. 'You do not know now what I am doing but later you will understand.'

'You will never wash my feet,' Peter said as Jesus knelt at his feet with the bowl.

Jesus smiled at him. 'Unless I wash you, you have no share in me.'

The atmosphere changed. Peter held up his hands: 'Lord not my feet only but my hands and my head as well.'

Jesus laughed then. 'One who has bathed does not need to wash except for the feet but is entirely clean. And you are clean – though not all of you.'

The washing went on. It took around half an hour for Jesus to get round everyone. All of us knew something had changed inside after the washing.

All except Judas – but that's another story.

Because of that washing we knew, deep down inside, more than we'd ever known before, that he loved us.

We knew we weren't perfect. But we knew we were forgiven.

And we knew we could be forgiven again and again.

And we understood what he was trying to teach us before he said it. Right at the end he went back to his place and he put the towel and the basin in the centre of the table.

'If I your Lord and teacher have washed your feet, you also ought to wash one another's feet. For I have set you an example that you also should do as I have done to you.'

People don't always understand what that means. Jesus was telling us to be humble and serve each other. But that wasn't the whole story.

Washing our feet was a sign of forgiveness. It was a sign that he forgave us and he loved us anyway. He was making us new.

By telling us to wash each other's feet, he was telling us something else as well: we had to forgive each other, not seven times but seventy times seven times.

That's what it means to follow him. It means being forgiven – and being ready to forgive.

Retold from John 13.1–20.

> 'The man called Jesus made mud, spread it on my
> eyes, and said to me, "Go to Siloam and wash."
> Then I went and washed and received my sight.'
>
> *John 9.11*

Sharing together

Share together in the act of washing the hands or the feet of the person sitting next to you.

You may want to do this in silence, giving thanks to God for the gift of forgiveness and praying for the strength to forgive others. You may want to listen to music or a Christian song as you wash one another's feet.

After the foot or hand washing, take some time to talk together about the foot washing story. What does it mean to you to be washed by Jesus and to be given the command to wash the feet of others?

Remember to keep the emphasis in your conversation on God's grace in washing our souls and forgiving our sins because of the death of Jesus on the cross. How deep is his love!

Part 3 Experiencing God's love through habits and practices

Take some time to reflect together on the habit and practice of confession and receiving God's forgiveness.

Public worship

What does this part of the service mean to you when we call to mind our sins, confess them to God and receive God's forgiveness. Here are three of the prayers used in the service of Holy Communion: the collect for purity and the prayer of humble access, followed by the absolution.

How do these prayers use the picture of being washed? What do they mean to you?

How can you best use the time when you first come into church and are waiting for the service to begin? How can you use the time after you have received Holy Communion?

> Almighty God,
> to whom all hearts are open,
> all desires known
> and from whom no secrets are hidden:
> cleanse the thoughts of our hearts
> by the inspiration of your Holy Spirit
> that we may perfectly love you
> and worthily magnify your holy name
> through Christ our LORD.
> **Amen.**

> We do not presume
> to come to this your table, merciful LORD
> trusting in our own righteousness
> but in your manifold and great mercies.
> We are not worthy
> so much as to gather up the crumbs under your table
> but you are the same LORD
> whose nature is always to have mercy.
> Grant us therefore, gracious LORD,
> so to eat the flesh of your dear son Jesus Christ
> and to drink his blood
> that our sinful bodies may be made clean by his body
> and our souls washed through his most precious blood
> and that we may evermore dwell in him and he in us.
> **Amen.**

> Almighty God,
> who forgives all who truly repent
> have mercy upon you
> pardon and deliver you from all your sins
> confirm and strengthen you in all goodness
> and keep you in life eternal
> through Jesus Christ our LORD.
> **Amen.**

*Prayer taken from the Order for the Celebration and Holy Communion, *Common Worship: Services and Prayers for the Church of England* (2000), copyright © The Archbishops' Council and is reproduced by permission.

Private prayer and Bible reading

How often does an examination of conscience, confession and the theme of being washed feature in your private prayers?

Some in the Anglican tradition find the practice of confession to a priest helpful at regular intervals or at particular moments of their lives.

For everyone, times and seasons of the year when we take time to examine ourselves and take stock of our growth in holiness and experience of God's love are important.

Lent and Advent are seasons of the year that can be used in this way. Take some time and space to be in a quiet place: in church or the place where you normally pray. Remember God's great love and mercy.

Use a passage of Scripture to help you reflect on your journey and the things you may need to confess or the people you may need to forgive.

Here are some passages of Scripture that may be helpful:

Exodus 20.1–17 – The ten commandments

Matthew 5.1–10 – The beatitudes

Romans 12.9–21 – Living in response to God's grace

1 Corinthians 13 – Christian love

Focus your reflections in two short lists. The first should be a list of words and actions you seek God's forgiveness for. The second should be a list of people whom you need to forgive in this season of your life.

Turn both lists into a prayer along the following lines:

Dear Father
I thank you for your love and grace in my life
Thank you for your washing and cleansing for my sins.
I confess to you the following and seek your forgiveness:

Use the list of sins here.

Have mercy on me, O God, according to your steadfast love
According to your great gentleness, wipe away my sins
Wash me through and through from my iniquity
And from all my sins please make me clean. Amen.

Almighty Father
You call us to forgive others their sins as you forgive us
In your name I now forgive:

Use the list of people you need to forgive here.

> Give me grace to live in the strength you give and to wash the feet of others
> Through Jesus Christ our LORD. Amen.

For discussion

● Which of these habits and practices will you pay attention to in the coming year?

● What new insights about God's love are you taking away from this session?

Prayers together

Before you pray, spend a few moments in quietness and rest, thinking back to the foot washing.

> Have mercy on me, O God, according to your steadfast love
> **According to your great gentleness, wipe away my sins**
>
> Wash me through and through from my iniquity
> **And from all my sins please make me clean**
>
> For I know my transgressions all too well
> **My sin is before my eyes continually**
>
> Against you and you alone I have sinned
> **I have done great evil in your sight**
>
> Therefore you are right to pass sentence on me
> **And accurate in your judgement**
>
> Truly I was conceived in iniquity
> **In sin did my mother conceive me**
>
> Truly it is truth you long for deep within
> **So in my secret heart please teach me wisdom**
>
> Purge me with hyssop and I shall be clean
> **Wash me and I shall be whiter than snow**
>
> Let me hear joy and celebration again
> **Let the bones you have crushed rejoice**
>
> Turn away your face from my sins
> **Hide all of my iniquities**

A clean heart create in me, O God,
An upright spirit set deep within me.

Psalm 51.1–10

A time of open prayer or one person may lead prepared intercessions.

Pray for one another and for any questions that have arisen.

Pray for one another in your intention to build good habits of forgiving others and being forgiven.

End with the Lord's Prayer introduced by:

Trusting in the compassion of God,
As our Saviour taught us so we pray:
Our Father in heaven …

Now, LORD, you let your servant go in peace;
Your word has been fulfilled.

My own eyes have seen the salvation
Which you have prepared in the sight of every people.

A light to reveal you to the nations
And the glory of your people Israel.

Glory to the Father and to the Son
And to the Holy Spirit
**As it was in the beginning, is now
And shall be for ever. Amen.**

The Song of Simeon

Bless the LORD, O my soul,
And all that is within me bless his holy name

Bless the LORD, O my soul,
And forget not all his benefits

Who forgives all your sins
And heals all your infirmities

Who redeems your life from the Pit
And crowns you with faithful love and compassion

Who satisfies you with good things
So that your youth is renewed like an eagle's.

Psalm 103.1–5

For reflection and practice by group members after the session

- Write down the steps you need to take to build the good habits you explored in the session.

- Take one practical step in this direction.

ENLIGHTENED

notes for group leaders

Approximate timings for the session are:

Welcome; opening prayers and reflection	15 mins
Sharing your story	15 mins
Film or song clip	5 mins
A testimony (reading and reflection)	10 mins
Sharing together	20 mins
Habits and practices	15 mins
Final worship and prayers together	10 mins

There is a lot of material in each session so you will need to select from week to week.

Additional activities

The activity for the session centres on lighting candles. You need to make sure the room can be darkened if it is still light outside. You will need a low table and a collection of candles of different sizes – two or three for every member of the group.

Some of the candles should be on plates or saucers so they can be passed around the group at the end of the session. You will also need matches and a taper.

Make sure the room is a safe one in which to light candles and have some water or sand ready in case a candle is knocked over.

There is a short sound file on the Church House Publishing website which introduces the session. If you decide to use this, it can be played after the initial reading of the psalm. To find the clip go to **www.chpublishing.co.uk/experiencinggodslove** and follow the link.

Involving the group

You may want to involve different members of the group in:

- Leading the opening and closing worship.
- Providing the equipment for the candle lighting and the refreshments.
- Reading the story.

Ideas for film clips and music tracks

There is a very good scene in 'Harry Potter and the Order of the Phoenix', where Harry confronts the Dementors in an underpass which illustrates the theme of light overcoming darkness.

The song 'Light of the World' by Matt Redman would be a good one to play at the beginning or the end of the session.

You will need a recording of the Taizé song, 'The Lord is my light', for the practical exercise.

Advance notice for next week

The activity is the making of collages. It would be a help if people could bring magazines and newspapers and other materials.

ENLIGHTENED

Begin with the opening prayers on page 9.

The LORD is my light and my salvation. Whom shall I fear?
**The LORD is the strong safe place of my life. Why should
I tremble?**

When the wicked surround me to devour my flesh
My enemies and foes will stumble and fall

If I face whole armies my heart will not be afraid
If I fight great battles I will be bold and strong.

One thing I have asked from the LORD and one thing I seek
**To dwell in the house of the LORD all the days of my life.
To ponder the LORD'S beauty and to wonder in his temple.**

For he will hide me in his shelter in the day of trouble
He will conceal me in the cover of his tent
On rock he will set me on high.

Now my head is lifted high above my enemies and foes
**I will offer sacrifices in his tent – a sacrifice of praise
I will sing and make music to the LORD.**

Hear, O LORD, the call of my heart
Be gracious to me. Answer me.

'Come,' says my heart. 'Seek his face.'
Your face I seek, O LORD.

Do not turn your face from me
Do not turn your servant away in anger
You are my life's helper.

cont. on p.52

> Though my father and my mother forsake me
> **The LORD will bear me up.**
>
> Teach me, O LORD, your ways
> **And lead me on a level path**
> **For my enemies are many.**
>
> Do not give me up to the will of my foes
> **For false witnesses rise up against me breathing violence.**
>
> I trust that I will see the goodness of the LORD in the land
> of life.
> **Wait for the LORD**
> **Be strong and take courage in your heart. Wait for the LORD.**
>
> *Psalm 27*

Part 1 Experiencing God's love through the psalm

When my younger son was about to get married, we hosted his stag party at our house. The highlight of the weekend was a night hike. The boys divided into two teams and each was given a map and asked to select the most remote spot they could find within a six-mile radius as the starting point for the other team. Both teams were blindfolded and taken by car to the selected location. They unloaded at the dead of night with a map but no idea where they were. Mobile phones were turned off. The first one to make it back to the house won the race.

Actually it wasn't that difficult. It was a clear night. Although the hills around Sheffield are very high, it's not very hard to work out where the city is: it glows well into the night. From that they could work out their direction and then it wasn't too hard to find their way home. Even so, that one night hike was enough to give a taste of darkness and what it can mean.

The psalmist sings: The LORD is my light and my salvation. The writers of this psalm have experienced God's love as light piercing the darkness, shining constantly and steadily, chasing away all fear.

Psalm 27 is a deeply personal psalm. Throughout God is called by his own personal name – a name so holy it is never pronounced aloud by the Jews. In

English, the name is sometimes written as Yahweh and sometimes as LORD in capital letters. But it means much more than LORD. To use the word means to be on first name terms with God, as it were. A Christian can catch some of the sense of intimacy by reading the psalm and substituting the name Jesus where the psalm has LORD. Try it and see.

Psalm 27 is written from a curious place. Look and see how the psalm moves between confidence and trust on the one hand and anxious prayer for God's help on the other. Some of the psalms are written from a place of complete trust, such as Psalm 23 which we will study in the next session. Some psalms begin from a place of feeling abandoned by God, such as Psalm 22, and reach a better place by the end. This psalm begins with some beautiful statements of trust and confidence, but as it unfolds we hear also real cries for strength and help. Some scholars think that the first six verses were originally a separate psalm of trust (down to 'make music to the Lord') and this longer more anxious prayer has been woven onto it.

Whatever the origins of the psalm, the words we are given help us to pray especially in those moments when we are in conflict within ourselves and there is a battle going on between our trust in God and our fear of life. Many, many people in our world do battle on a daily basis with all kinds of fear and anxiety. We have many different names for phobias – you can probably think of some. For some people, the whole idea that a Christian can be afraid or gripped by fear is strange. Isn't it simply a matter of trusting in God? Well, for some it is. But for others, the battle is one to be fought and overcome each day. Psalm 27 lets us see inside that battle.

Like Psalm 103, this psalm helps us to talk to our own hearts and to dialogue with ourselves. Through the words of the psalm we remember God's help in times past when God has rescued or delivered us. The words of the psalm help us to listen to our own hearts – to the deepest longings within us:

> 'Come,' says my heart. 'Seek his face.'
> Your face I seek, O LORD.
>
> *Psalm 27.7*

Psalm 27 gives us profound words of confidence in moments of fear and difficulty to speak to our own souls as in the final verse:

> I trust that I will see the goodness of the LORD in the land of life.
> Wait for the LORD;
> Be strong and take courage in your heart. Wait for the LORD.
>
> *Psalm 27.13–14*

There is no single form of trouble in view. Reference is made to physical danger in battle; to hurtful words spoken; to the lawcourts. For that reason the words of the psalm are a help and comfort in just about any difficult circumstances. Like the other psalms in this series, it is worth learning by heart the verses that particularly strike you.

Although there are many beautiful verses and images in this one psalm, the first few words are the most striking of all:

> 'The LORD is my light and my salvation. Whom shall I fear?'
>
> *Psalm 27.1*

The image of light as an image for God runs right through the Scriptures. In the story of creation at the beginning of Genesis, the earth was a formless void and darkness covered the face of the deep. This dark void is the place where fear dwells. Creation begins when God says: 'Let there be light.' The very first act in creation is the making of light shining out of darkness. The final book of the Bible, Revelation, ends with a glorious vision of the City of God, the new Jerusalem, coming down from heaven. The city has no need of any kind of light:

> For the glory of God is its light, and its lamp is the Lamb.
>
> *Revelation 21.23*

In this city, nothing is allowed that will make you afraid.

When Isaiah is searching for a way to communicate the difference the Messiah will make, he reaches for the vocabulary of light and darkness:

> The people who walked in darkness have seen a great light;
> those who lived in a land of deep darkness –
> on them light has shined.
>
> *Isaiah 9.2*

The early chapters of Luke's Gospel are full of the theme of light. The Benedictus, the Song of Zechariah, unfolds the beautiful image of the coming of Jesus being like the dawn of a new day. Note the connection between light and love here:

> 'By the tender mercy of our God, the dawn from on high shall break upon us,
> to give light to those who sit in darkness and the shadow of death.'
>
> *Luke 1.78–79*

In the Song of Simeon, the revealing of the Messiah in the baby Jesus is 'A light for revelation to the Gentiles and for glory to your people Israel' (Luke 2.32). I am told that in the Portuguese language, the words for giving birth mean literally, bring light, which echoes the same kind of idea.

But it is John's Gospel, of course, that picks up the theme from Psalm 27.1 most clearly and profoundly in the opening verses of the Gospel (verses that echo the creation story):

> What has come into being in him was life and the life was the light of all people. The light shines in the darkness, and the darkness did not overcome it.
>
> *John 1.3–5*

> The true light which enlightens everyone was coming into the world.
>
> *John 1.9*

John uses the picture of light and darkness to illustrate the reason some did not accept his message in his dialogue with Nicodemus:

> … the light has come into the world, and people loved darkness rather than light because their deeds were evil.
>
> *John 3.19*

And it is John of course who tells us of Jesus' own claim, a claim that can only be understood against the background of this Old Testament imagery and prophecy:

> 'I am the light of the world. Whoever follows me will never walk in darkness but will have the light of life.'
>
> *John 8.12*

Sometimes the image of the dawning of the light is used as a picture of the beginnings of Christian faith. When Saul is on the road to Damascus he sees a blinding light from heaven and he is enlightened in a life-changing way. But the picture is used more often as a picture for the way in which our way and our lives are illuminated by God's grace not just at the beginning of the journey but every step of the way.

Paul writes to the Corinthians, connecting the creation story with the way our lives are lit by grace:

For it is the God who said, 'Let light shine out of darkness', who has shone in our hearts to give the light of the knowledge of the glory of God in the face of Jesus Christ.

2 Corinthians 4.6

The verses that follow speak of the ongoing struggle of the Christian life. It is clear that this is a daily walk and a battle between the light of Christ and the fear in our hearts.

The letter to the Ephesians uses the image of light to describe the change that grows in the life of the Christian as our lives reflect the light we have ourselves been given. As God enlightens us so we slowly grow in holiness and become different from the world around us:

For once you were darkness but now in the LORD you are light. Live as children of light – for the fruit of light is found in all that is good and right and true. Try to find out what is pleasing to the LORD. Take no part in the unfruitful works of darkness, but instead expose them.

Ephesians 5.8–10

The first letter of John draws this out still further. If we share in God's nature (light rather than darkness) then our lives will reflect this truth in our actions: we will walk in the light. Here the picture of light is combined with the picture of being washed:

This is the message we have heard from him and proclaim to you, that God is light and in him there is no darkness at all. If we say that we have fellowship with him while we are walking in darkness, we lie and do not do what is true. But if we walk in the light as he himself is in the light, we have fellowship with one another, and the blood of his Son Jesus Christ cleanses us from all sin.

1 John 1.5

It seems simple to pray in the words of the psalmist: 'The LORD is my light and my salvation. Whom shall I fear?' Yet as we pray these words there are many things going on. There is a battle between God's light in our lives and the darkness of fear. There is a moral struggle as we choose to walk in the light rather than the darkness. There is grace at work as we receive God's light day by day, flooding our lives with love with every dawn, enabling us to live in him and for him each day.

Sharing your story

Share with one another the story of a time when you found yourself in the dark.

Which is your favourite verse from the psalm? Which will you try and learn by heart?

Where have you experienced God's light shining in your life? Was there a call to follow the light rather than the darkness in a particular choice you made? Was there a decision where you needed God's guidance? Is there a battle with some kind of fear?

You may want to share as a whole group; or one person might prepare in advance and tell part of their story; or you might want to share in twos or threes.

If you are reading this book on your own then take some time at this point to journal and look back on the way this sense of light and darkness has surfaced in your life.

A film or song clip

See page 50 for suggestions.

Part 2 Experiencing God's love through the Gospel of John

A testimony

Two people in the group should read the story aloud. It is a story for two voices – a man and a woman. The man speaks first.

> We did see what happened but we daren't say.
>
> *We've always wanted a quiet life, you see. Never wanted any trouble.*
>
> It was hard enough having a son like him.
>
> *We loved him. I always wanted a boy. He was my angel.*
>
> But he could never see. Completely blind. Right from birth.
>
> *He never knew any different. Never saw the light at all.*

Never saw sunshine or flowers. Never saw our faces even.

He managed alright when he was a boy.

The other children were cruel though. Not to mention the parents.

We lost friends as soon as he was born. They thought it was our fault he was blind. Something we'd done.

We'd done nothing, you understand. Nothing at all.

It was harder when he grew up. He couldn't do anything except beg.

We'd lead him out every morning to sit at the street corner and come and fetch him every night.

I dropped him off early in the morning that day.

That wonderful day.

Jesus came past. He was marvellous – but his disciples were like all the others.

'Who sinned – this man or his parents that he was born blind?'

'Neither this man nor his parents sinned' said Jesus.

Well we knew that. But it was still good to hear it from a Rabbi.

He said something else. I didn't catch it. Then he spat on the ground.

He made some mud and he spread the mud on our son's eyes. He didn't seem to mind.

I nearly stopped him then and there but he looked at me and smiled.

Then he told him to go to Siloam and wash off the mud. We took him there at once.

He was so excited he jumped into the water. He cupped his hands and poured it over his face.

Straight away he put his hands over his eyes. It was the light streaming in.

I called his name. He turn round and parted his fingers. He looked at us.

'Mum! Dad!' he said. 'I can see. The mud. It's healed me.'

'It was Jesus,' I said. 'It was the Rabbi, Jesus.'

Well there was no end of trouble. It was a Sabbath.

They asked him questions. They asked us questions. They wanted to know if he was really born blind. They wanted to know how he was healed.

We said nothing. We didn't want any more trouble. They were after him by then.

But nothing could shut him up, our son. He told them time and again: 'One thing I do know, that though I was blind now I see'.

It's still his favourite thing to say. Every day he tells us: 'One thing I do know, that though I was blind now I see.'

Jesus found him later – after they'd thrown him out of the temple. He found him and he became his follower.

So did we. From that day to this and for ever.

How could we not. Our son was blind and he could see.

He wasn't the only one. There was lots of blindness from that day to this.

Lots of blindness. But lots of light.

One thing I do know. Once I was blind but now I see.

Retold from John 9.1–41

> What has come into being in him was life, and the life was the light of all people.
>
> *John 1.3–4*

Sharing together

You will need an assortment of candles and candle holders for this activity. Set them on a low table in the middle of the room. Turn down the lights in the room so you sit in the semi-darkness.

Talk together about the story of the man born blind and his parents. What meaning do you find in the story?

Talk together about the darkness in the world. Take it in turns to mention specific instances. You may think about the darkness of ignorance; of evil; of confusion; of fear.

Light the first candle and begin the Taizé song based on Psalm 27.1: 'The Lord is my light and my salvation. In him I trust. In him I trust.'

You may want to listen to the song on CD or, if your group is musical, sing it together.

Take it in turns to light a candle. Each person who lights a candle should say:

The light of Christ shines in the darkness of ....

Continue until all the candles are lit.

Turn the lights on in the room but, if it is safe, leave the candles burning through the final discussion and prayers.

Part 3 Experiencing God's love through habits and practices

Jesus said, 'I am the light of the world' (John 8.12). Jesus also said 'You are the light of the world' (Matthew 5.14). Here is the passage in full:

> 'You are the light of the world. A city built on a hill cannot be hid. No one after lighting a lamp puts it under the bushel but on the lampstand and it gives light to all in the house. In the same way, let your light shine before others, so that they may see your good works and give glory to your Father in heaven.'
>
> *Matthew 5.14–16*

As the Lord gives light to our lives, so the challenge is to light the lives of others.

Take a very large sheet of paper and write on it some of the many different ways in which Christians you know are a light to the world. Which ones can you see in this group of people? What kind of actions and habits and practices can you think of that give light to the world.

Which ones do you feel called to begin or to develop in the coming year. How will you make a start? Share your good intentions with the whole group if you can.

For discussion

- Which of these habits and practices will you pay attention to in the coming year?

- What new insights about God's love are you taking away from this session?

Prayers together

Before you pray, spend a few moments in quietness and rest, thinking back to the lights shining in darkness. If it is safe to do so, pass the candles around so each member of the group holds a light.

The LORD is my light and my salvation. Whom shall I fear?
The LORD is the strong safe place of my life. Why should I tremble?

When the wicked surround me to devour my flesh
My enemies and foes will stumble and fall

If I face whole armies my heart will not be afraid
If I fight great battles I will be bold and strong.

One thing I have asked from the LORD and one thing I seek
To dwell in the house of the LORD all the days of my life.
To ponder the LORD'S beauty and to wonder in his temple.

For he will hide me in his shelter in the day of trouble
He will conceal me in the cover of his tent
On rock he will set me on high.

Now my head is lifted high above my enemies and foes
I will offer sacrifices in his tent – a sacrifice of praise
I will sing and make music to the LORD.

Hear, O LORD, the call of my heart
Be gracious to me. Answer me.

'Come,' says my heart. 'Seek his face.'
Your face I seek, O LORD.

Do not turn your face from me
Do not turn your servant away in anger
You are my life's helper.

Though my father and my mother forsake me
The LORD will bear me up.

Teach me, O LORD, your ways
And lead me on a level path
For my enemies are many.

Do not give me up to the will of my foes
For false witnesses rise up against me breathing violence.

I trust that I will see the goodness of the LORD in the land of life.
Wait for the LORD
Be strong and take courage in your heart. Wait for the LORD.

Psalm 27

A time of open prayer or one person may lead prepared intercessions.

Pray for one another and for any questions that have arisen.

Pray for one another in your intention to build good habits.

End with the Lord's Prayer introduced by:

Trusting in the compassion of God,
As our Saviour taught us so we pray:
Our Father in heaven ...

Now, LORD, you let your servant go in peace;
Your word has been fulfilled.

My own eyes have seen the salvation
Which you have prepared in the sight of every people.

A light to reveal you to the nations
And the glory of your people Israel.

Glory to the Father and to the Son
And to the Holy Spirit
As it was in the beginning, is now
And shall be for ever. Amen.

The Song of Simeon

Bless the LORD, O my soul,
And all that is within me bless his holy name

Bless the LORD, O my soul,
And forget not all his benefits

Who forgives all your sins
And heals all your infirmities

Who redeems your life from the Pit
And crowns you with faithful love and compassion

Who satisfies you with good things
So that your youth is renewed like an eagle's.

Psalm 103.1–5

For reflection and practice by group members after the session

● Write down the steps you need to take to build the good habits you explored in the session.

● Take one practical step in this direction.

TENDED

notes for leaders

Approximate timings for the session are:

Welcome; opening prayers and reflection	15 mins
Sharing your story	15 mins
Film or song clip	5 mins
A testimony (reading and reflection)	10 mins
Sharing together	20 mins
Habits and practices	15 mins
Final worship and prayers together	10 mins

There is a lot of material in each session so you will need to select from week to week.

Additional activities

The activity for the session is making collages. You will need a collection of magazines and newspapers together with some card, scissors and glue.
It would be very helpful if some of the magazines had pictures of sheep!

There is also an additional activity which involves making lists together so some flipchart paper and pens would be helpful together with anything that will help people bring to mind the different ways in which the church extends love and care (such as a parish magazine or news-sheet).

There is a short sound file on the Church House Publishing website which introduces the session. If you decide to use this, it can be played after the initial reading of the psalm. To find the clip go to **www.chpublishing.co.uk/experiencinggodslove** and follow the link.

Involving the group

You may want to involve different members of the group in:

- Leading the opening and closing worship.
- Providing the equipment for the activity and the refreshments.
- Reading the story.

Ideas for film clips and music tracks

The opening sequence of the animated film, 'Up!', is a very beautiful summary of the different phases of a man's life in the span of just a few minutes.

The hymn 'The King of Love my shepherd is' is a very well-known Christian reworking of Psalm 23. The Stuart Townend song, 'The Lord is my shepherd', is a similar contemporary song.

Advance notice for next week

The activity next week is a bring and share meal. You will need to make the necessary arrangements at the end of this session.

SESSION 4

TENDED

Begin with the opening prayers on page 9.

> The LORD is my shepherd.
> **I lack nothing at all**
>
> In green pastures he tends me.
> **By still waters he guides me.**
>
> My soul he restores to itself
> **He leads me in right pathways for his name's sake**
>
> Even if I walk in the valley of the shadow of death
> I will fear no evil
> **For you are with me.**
> **Your rod and your staff comfort me**
>
> You spread a table before me in the face of my foes
> **You have anointed my head with oil. My cup overflows.**
>
> Surely goodness and mercy will follow me all the days of my life
> **And I will dwell in the house of the LORD to the end of days.**
>
> *Psalm 23*

Part 1 Experiencing God's love through the psalm

Psalm 23 is from beginning to end a song of trust and confidence. In Psalm 27, as we saw, there is a battle between trust and anxiety from the opening verse. In Psalm 23 the sense of confidence is there right from the start. The psalm does not give us a perfect picture of the world. The psalmist's soul needs to be restored. There is a deep dark valley to be faced. There are enemies all around.

But the song gives us words of trust and confidence in the face of difficulty, which is why these words have been cherished from generation to generation for thousands of years.

Psalm 23 is best seen as a kind of creed: a declaration of faith and trust. It is not really a song of praise. Nor is it a prayer: God is not asked to do anything. Instead, through the whole seven verses the psalm gives voice to a deep inner confidence in the personal love of God (note that God's name is again used as in Psalm 27). The psalm uses not one but two beautiful pictures of that love. The first is the image of the shepherd which runs through verses 1 to 4. The second is the equally powerful image of God as host, the one who welcomes us to a banquet, in verses 5 and 6.

The first three verses talk about God in the third person: 'The LORD is my shepherd.' The next two speak directly to God in the second person: 'You are with me ... your rod and staff comfort me ... you spread a table before me ... you anoint my head with oil.' The final verse sums up the theme of the psalm in the first person: 'I will dwell in the house of the LORD to the end of days.' From beginning to end the psalm is about being tended by the Lord: loved and looked after in every part of life's journey.

From time to time all of us must ask the question: what is the point of being a Christian? It is a way of life that is often difficult and sacrificial. It can be hard to sustain the walk of faith from year to year and through each chapter of our lives. From time to time others will ask us that question as well. Fellow Christians may ask us in times of difficulty or weariness: what is the point? Those who are not Christians may ask us in genuine enquiry: what is the reason for your faith?

There are many ways to answer the question to ourselves or others but these beautiful images from the psalms give us some insights at least. To be a Christian means that our lives can be deeply rooted in the life of God. Those roots bring steadiness and stability to our own lives and our family and they enable us over the seasons of our lives to bear fruit. To be a Christian means that we come to God's love for a washing and cleansing of our past mistakes and present faults. We have the ways and means to make new beginnings and because of that to forgive others also and make a fresh start with them. To be a Christian means that we are not living our lives in the darkness of ignorance or confusion or fear. The Lord himself is the light of our lives. His guidance to us and presence within us lights up the way. To be a Christian means that we are not living our lives in isolation. The Lord himself tends us and guides us in all the different circumstances of the journey from the very beginning to the very end.

As ever, we need to read Psalm 23 and the image of the shepherd against the background of its time. The picture of a shepherd is commonly used in the Ancient Near East and in the Old Testament as a picture for a king or other ruler of the nation. Ezekiel 34 contains a long prophecy against the shepherds (or rulers) of Israel. In the second part of Isaiah, the Persian king Cyrus is called a shepherd (Isaiah 44.28). David, the founder of the great dynasty which ruled Israel and Judah for hundreds of years, was, according the stories in Samuel, a shepherd boy. There is a close association between many of the psalms and the person of the king playing his part in the temple worship (look back to Psalms 20 and 21 for some examples). It seems likely that Psalm 23 was intended in some way to be a prayer of the King: as the King is the shepherd of God's people, so the King acknowledges that the Lord is his personal shepherd.

The link between the shepherd and kingship is important for another reason. The image of God as Shepherd is about more than tender loving care when we are in need. The image is also about God's guidance and reign and governance in our lives. In that sense, confessing that 'The LORD is my Shepherd' is not so different from saying 'Jesus is Lord'. We are placing ourselves within God's kingdom and authority and acknowledging God's rule in our own lives.

This in turn leads us to the truth that human life is not meant to be lived in independence from God's authority. We are created by God to live in communion with God himself and to acknowledge his rule or reign over our lives. One of the great lessons of ancient Israel to the world is that power can only be safely exercised in human affairs when the rulers are themselves subject to a higher authority: the authority of God himself. Whatever authority we are given in human affairs, we need to see ourselves as subject to God's just and gentle reign and his authority in our lives. We see the drama of power corrupting played out today in our own political life. But what is true on a larger scale in the affairs of nations is true also in our own lives. We live best when we live within the framework of a higher authority outside ourselves – the authority of God's love.

How does the Shepherd's care work out in our own lives? The images in the psalm affirm God's love first of all in the provision of all we need to sustain lives: food and drink. A shepherd leads his sheep on constantly to rich pasture. To be tended by the Lord means to be ready always to move on in our journey to a place where we can be fed and nurtured. One commentator refers to the shepherd's practice of turning tiny streams into pools of water where sheep can drink by creating dams from stones and gathering places. For the Christian, we trust God's provision, in the words of the Lord's Prayer, for our daily bread:

physical food but also spiritual food for the journey – words that connect us to the image of God spreading a meal at the end of the psalm.

In the rush of our world and many of our lives, there is something very powerful in the picture of green pastures and still waters. Those images for us summon up pictures of rest, retreat and recreation. There is something very unhurried about the first few verses of Psalm 23. Trusting in God in deeper and deeper ways should lead us to a more confident way of living which is able to slow down, avoid frantic business and pace ourselves well. For many of us that is a constant challenge.

That sense of restoration is carried forward into the next image caught in the phrase: 'My soul he restores to itself.' Underlying this image, perhaps, is the theme of Sabbath in the Scriptures. One of God's commandments to men and women is that we rest. Specifically, God commands that we build patterns and rhythms of rest into our lives. This is so important that the theme of Sabbath rest is built into the story of creation in Genesis 2 and makes it into the Ten Commandments. Weaving rest into the tapestry of our lives and finding sustainable rhythms of rest, prayer and work is potentially such good news for our 24/7 culture. It is also an area where many Christians need help and need God's tending.

There is a strong sense in the psalm of God guiding and leading the community and the individual Christian. The passage from Romans 12, which we are using each week in the opening prayers, stresses that every Christian brings unique gifts and qualities to God's service. These verses also affirm that each Christian has their own calling, their own vocation. God guides us into right pathways. This means first that we are given as Christians, wise instruction on how to live our lives in a way that is righteous, honest and just. However, it also means that God, by his Spirit, will guide us at the different key junctions in our lives. This guidance happens as we listen to the wisdom of others; as we pray and seek the path of peace in each situation; and sometimes as we listen for God's still small voice speaking within us as we look for the next step.

The shepherd's role is to tend: to nurture, to heal, to guide and also to protect. Sheep in the wilderness have natural enemies. The shepherd David describes the way he had to defend the flock against lions and bears (1 Samuel 17.34). The psalmist knows that we inhabit a dangerous and difficult world. We can never avoid suffering, difficulty or death. But that suffering, difficulty and death are transformed by the presence of the Lord. Some of the English versions smooth away the phrase 'The valley of the shadow of death' which is the literal Hebrew translation of verse 4. NRSV has 'darkest valley'. Yet the image and the older translations are one of the very reasons why the psalm has become such a powerful text. Psalm 23 acknowledges the bitter reality of death and bereavement. The psalm does not yet point forward to resurrection. Yet it does affirm the powerful truth of God's presence even at the ending of life.

In just a few verses, Psalm 23 captures and affirms a sense of God's abiding presence with us through times of rest and recreation, in our journeys, in all our comings and goings, at life's beginning, middle and at its close.

However, from a Christian perspective, we have only begun to explore its meaning. We have already seen the way in which in John's Gospel Jesus uses many of these images of transformation and applies them to himself. Psalm 1 summons us to be rooted in the Word of God. In John's Gospel, Jesus is the living Word and he says of himself: 'I am the vine, you are the branches.' The disciples are summoned to abide – or be firmly rooted – in the vine. Psalm 51 calls us to be washed, cleansed and refreshed in our journey through life. In John's Gospel, Jesus calls us to be born of water and the Spirit (3.5). Jesus offers to the Samaritan woman the gift of living water (4.10). Psalm 27.1 declares in confidence: 'The LORD is my light and salvation.' In John's Gospel Jesus declares: 'I am the Light of the World' (8.12).

Psalm 23 gives us words to declare in trust and confidence: The LORD is my shepherd. In John 10 Jesus declares (twice in succession) 'I am the good shepherd':

> 'I am the good shepherd. The good shepherd lays down his life for the sheep. The hired hand, who is not the shepherd and does not own the sheep, sees the wolf coming and leaves the sheep and runs away – and the wolf snatches them and scatters them. The hired hand runs away because a hired hand does not care for the sheep. I am the good shepherd. I know my own and my own know me, just as the Father knows me and I know the Father. And I lay down my life for the sheep. I have other sheep that do not belong to this fold. I must bring them also, and they will listen to my voice. So there will be one flock, one shepherd.'
>
> *John 10.11–16*

As with the other images, Jesus here takes all that is in the picture from the psalms and applies it to himself but then adds other layers of meaning. Because Jesus declares, 'I am the good shepherd', the Christian can read Psalm 23 and declare with confidence: 'Jesus the Lord is my shepherd.' That picture carries with it all the meanings we have already explored in the shepherd's tending of his sheep: nurture, rest, healing, governance, guidance and protection. The picture is, again, a royal picture. A shepherd is a king in Israel. Jesus is claiming clearly and directly to be God's anointed King, or Messiah, who has come to bring a new kingdom, the reign of heaven on earth.

However, Jesus adds a vital new dimension to the picture here, founded on love. That vital new dimension is that the shepherd lays down his life for the sheep. This is repeated three times (vv. 11, 15, 17) and is the central theme of the passage. Note that Jesus does not simply say: 'I risk my life for the sheep.' A very good shepherd may occasionally have to do that. He says: 'I lay down my life for the sheep.' Jesus makes an offering of his own life. To be the good shepherd means he must sacrifice himself and go to his death. This makes Jesus the opposite of a normal human shepherd who will sacrifice his sheep so that he can live. Jesus goes willingly to his death so that we might have the gift of life.

And the motive for this great act of sacrifice? Nothing else but love – and love that is founded on a close and personal knowledge of each of the flock. Through the image, Jesus begins to build the profound picture of uniting in himself a flock drawn from many different languages, nations and places to be one flock and one shepherd.

Sharing your story

Share with one another the different ways you feel you have experienced God's guidance through the years.

Which verse of the psalm means most to you and why?

When did you first become aware that Jesus Christ died for you and what that must mean for your life?

You may want to share as a whole group; or one person might prepare in advance and tell part of their story; or you might want to share in twos or threes.

If you are reading this book on your own then take some time at this point to journal and look back on the way this sense of being tended has surfaced in your life.

A film or song clip

See page 66 for suggestions.

Part 2 Experiencing God's love through the Gospel of John

A testimony

One of the group should read the story aloud.

> There's an old negro spiritual you love to sing at Passiontide:
> 'Were you there when they crucified my Lord?'
>
> Well, I was there. I was his friend – the one he loved. I'd
> followed him for years. At first I followed because of all the
> hope he represented. Then that hope turned to understanding.
> I knew he was the Messiah. That knowledge was tested over
> and over again in his teaching and in the signs he did. The whole
> world could not contain what Jesus said and did.
>
> Then that understanding turned to love. He was my friend.
>
> Most of the others scattered after the arrest. They were
> ashamed afterwards. Even so, many of them ended up sharing
> this kind of death. I don't know what made me different.
> I couldn't turn away somehow. So I followed and watched.
> His mother was there and so were some of the other women.
>
> He carried the cross out to the Place of the Skull. You know the
> story. He was crucified there between two thieves. It was a
> horrible death. It's not like some of the pictures. The place was
> filthy. People passed by shouting insults. Those who were
> crucified were meant to be an example – to keep us all in fear.
> It was a criminal's death.
>
> The Romans put the sign above his head, King of the Jews.
> That annoyed the priests I can tell you. It was never more true
> than on that day.
>
> You know the details of the story, I'm sure. People have tried to
> imagine it all over the world. To watch him die for me was so
> very painful. I would rather have been crucified myself than see
> it happen to him. He was my friend. He was my King.
>
> He asked me to take care of his mother. She was with me until
> the end.

I expect you know his final words: 'It is finished'. The great work was accomplished. This was the task he came to fulfil. This was the heart of it really: laying down his life for his friends. This was the moment in which the world was redeemed.

We had no idea at the time of course. We were encouraged a little by his sense of purpose. He always knew exactly what he was doing. But we were overwhelmed with grief as well.

They took him down. We watched as he was laid in the tomb. Three days later we would only begin to understand.

Retold from John 19.16–30

> No one has greater love than this: to lay down his life for his friends.
>
> *John 15.13*

Sharing together

Divide into pairs and using the magazines and other materials provided make a collage to depict the themes of Psalm 23.

As you work together, talk about the different ways in which you have experienced God's tending in your life through its different times and seasons.

What does the death of Jesus on the cross mean to you?

Spend a little time talking about the collages with one another at the end.

Part 3 Experiencing God's love through habits and practices

Jesus the good shepherd laid down his life for the sheep. The same Jesus says to his disciples:

'Love one another as I have loved you.'

John 13.34

The Christian Church has always been a place where people are tended in all the ways described in Psalm 23.

Take some time to list together the different ways in which your local church extends love and care to the congregation and to those outside the congregation. Make an actual list on a large piece of paper. Some of them will be informal and some will be formal.

You may want to think of the themes of the psalm: nurture; healing; rest; protection and hospitality.

Make another list of the particular gifts and resources the members of your group bring or could bring to that work of tending and loving one another. It might be a personal quality or a gift of encouragement or the gift of time.

What are the ways in which the members of the group could develop the habits and practices of tending and caring for others in the coming year?

For discussion

● Which of these habits and practices will you pay attention to in the coming year?

● What new insights about God's love are you taking away from this session?

Prayers together

Before you pray, spend a few moments in quietness and rest. Put the collages and lists in the centre of the room where everyone can see them.

> The LORD is my shepherd.
> **I lack nothing at all**
>
> In green pastures he tends me.
> **By still waters he guides me.**
>
> My soul he restores to itself
> **He leads me in right pathways for his name's sake**
>
> Even if I walk in the valley of the shadow of death
> I will fear no evil
> **For you are with me.**
> **Your rod and your staff comfort me**
>
> You spread a table before me in the face of my foes
> **You have anointed my head with oil. My cup overflows.**

Surely goodness and mercy will follow me all the days of my life
And I will dwell in the house of the LORD to the end of days.

Psalm 23

A time of open prayer or one person may lead prepared intercessions.

Pray for one another and for any questions that have arisen.

Pray for one another in your intention to build good habits of forgiving others and being forgiven.

End with the Lord's Prayer introduced by:

Trusting in the compassion of God,
As our Saviour taught us so we pray:
Our Father in heaven ...

Now, LORD, you let your servant go in peace;
Your word has been fulfilled.

My own eyes have seen the salvation
Which you have prepared in the sight of every people.

A light to reveal you to the nations
And the glory of your people Israel.

Glory to the Father and to the Son
And to the Holy Spirit
As it was in the beginning, is now
And shall be for ever. Amen.

The Song of Simeon

Bless the LORD, O my soul,
And all that is within me bless his holy name

Bless the LORD, O my soul,
And forget not all his benefits

Who forgives all your sins
And heals all your infirmities

Who redeems your life from the Pit
And crowns you with faithful love and compassion

Who satisfies you with good things
So that your youth is renewed like an eagle's.

Psalm 103.1–5

For reflection and practice by group members after the session

- Write down the steps you need to take to build the good habits you explored in the session.

- Take one practical step in this direction.

WELCOMED

Approximate timings for the session are:

Welcome; opening prayers and reflection	15 mins
Sharing your story	15 mins
Film or song clip	5 mins
A testimony (reading and reflection)	10 mins
Sharing together	20 mins
Habits and practices	15 mins
Final worship and prayers together	10 mins

There is a lot of material in each session so you will need to select from week to week.

Additional activities

The activity for the session is simply sharing a meal together as a celebration of the life of your group over the last five weeks.

In most situations it will be best if this is a simple bring and share meal. Alternatively you might want to ask someone to provide a main course and other people to bring salads and puddings. It will need organizing the week before, of course.

There is a short sound file on the Church House Publishing website which introduces the session. If you decide to use this, it can be played after the

initial reading of the psalm. To find the clip go to
www.chpublishing.co.uk/experiencinggodslove and follow the link.

Involving the group

You may want to involve different members of the group in:

- Leading the opening and closing worship.
- Providing the food for the meal.
- Reading the story.

Ideas for film clips and music tracks

The Channel 4 TV series 'Come Dine with Me' is immensely popular at the present time and involves a competition where four people in the same town invite each other to a meal and then give points for different aspects of the evening. Find a five-minute clip from this to illustrate some aspect of hospitality.

The old hymn 'O welcome all you noble saints of old' touches on many of the themes of this session as does the modern song, 'Broken for me'.

There are one or two very good videos of 'God and man at table are sat down' on YouTube.

Following on from the group

You may want to give some thought to how the group follows on from these five sessions in advance of your meeting.

WELCOMED

notes for group leaders

Begin with the opening prayers on page 9.

Guard me, O God, for I have put my trust in you
I say to you, O LORD: You are my LORD
I have no good apart from you

I say to the holy ones who are in the land
And to their leaders: All my delight is in them

Those who choose another God multiply their sorrows
I will not pour out their offerings of blood
I will not speak their name with my lips

The LORD is my choice portion and my cup
You continue to be my lot

The boundary lines have fallen for me in good places
There is a good inheritance for me

I bless the LORD who counsels me
In the night also he instructs my heart

I keep the LORD before me always
Because he is at my right hand I shall not be moved

Therefore my heart rejoices and my inner being shouts for joy
My flesh also rests secure

For you have not forsaken my soul to Sheol
You have not allowed your holy one to see destruction

You show me the path of life. Fullness of joy is in your presence
Pleasures for evermore are at your right hand.

Psalm 16

Part 1 Experiencing God's love through the psalm

All through the Scriptures there is an interplay between the two images of guest and host. Normally it is God who is the host and we are the guest but from time to time the image is reversed. In the garden of Eden, the first man and the first woman are God's guests and tenants. They enjoy paradise at God's invitation. Later in Genesis, in the story of the visit of the three travellers to Abraham, it is God himself who is the guest and Abraham who is the host.

In the Exodus from Egypt, God commands the Israelites to remember the night they were given their freedom in a special meal: the Passover, which continues to this day. In the journey through the wilderness it is God who leads his people like a shepherd and feeds them through the gifts of manna, quails and water.

The temple, like all temples in the ancient world, is simply called God's house. It is seen as God's home and we come there as guests invited to a feast. The term sacrifice in English means primarily to give up something that is costly and that idea is certainly present in the Old Testament. But a sacrifice at one of the great festivals was also a special meal eaten in or near God's house and in his presence.

In the Book of Proverbs, divine Wisdom is portrayed as someone who builds a house and invites people to come to the feast:

> Come, eat of my bread and drink of the wine I have mixed
> Lay aside immaturity and live
> And walk in the way of insight.
>
> *Proverbs 9.5–6*

In the prophetic tradition, there are wonderful stories of God feeding the prophet Elijah in the wilderness (1 Kings 19): tending and welcome intertwine. In Isaiah 55, God gives a wonderful invitation to all who will come to dine at his table:

> Ho, everyone who thirsts, come to the waters;
> And you that have no money, come, buy and eat!
> Come, buy wine and milk without money and without price.
>
> *Isaiah 55.1–2*

The picture of God as the host of the banquet from Psalm 23 fits into this broader tradition. The Lord is the one who welcomes us to the feast in his presence and in his house. This is not a meal we prepare. This is God's banquet and we are his guests:

You prepare a table before me in the presence of my enemies
You anoint my head with oil; my cup overflows
Surely goodness and mercy shall follow me all the days of my life
And I shall dwell in the house of the LORD my whole life long.

Psalm 23.5–6

Psalm 16 echoes some of this imagery. The psalm is another song of confidence like Psalms 27 and 23. In this psalm the emphasis is on devotion to God and choosing loyalty to the Lord in the face of temptation to offer sacrifices – or share in the meals – to other gods.

The picture of the meal is extended even further in verse 5:

The LORD is my choice portion and my cup.

There is a double symbolism in the Hebrew here. The picture in these verses in part echoes the distribution of the land to the Israelites by lot after the conquest of Canaan. The second half of the verse and the following verse about boundary lines draw on this memory. The emphasis is that the Lord himself is enough. But the reference to sacrifices and offerings in the previous verse also mean that the picture of the temple sacrifice and imagery is in view. The word 'portion' can also mean a portion of food or an allotted portion of the sacrifice. The psalm is saying here, in part, that not only is the Lord our host. He is also the meal: the food and the drink we share.

These are big statements. Think about them carefully. The Lord is the land where we live. The Lord is the host of our lives. The Lord is our very food and drink.

In Psalm 16, trust and confidence build from beginning to end and no wonder. If we are able to catch a vision of God as the ground of our being, the one who welcomes us to his table in love, the one who is himself our food and our nourishment then we will live our lives in confidence and trust and also in joy.

Psalm 16 and Psalm 23 both strain forward, as it were, to a relationship with God which might endure beyond death. Psalm 23 attempts to put this into words in the final verse. Psalm 16.11 is clearer:

You show me the path of life.
Fullness of joy is in your presence.
Pleasures for evermore are at your right hand.

There is no clear concept of life after death in the Old Testament but the psalmists and the prophets wrestle with the dilemma of the great love of God and the goodness of life on the one hand and the finality of death on the other.

They are inspired by the Spirit to look forward to a time when death itself will be defeated and God's presence can be enjoyed for evermore. All of these ideas come together in a wonderful vision from the Book of Isaiah. There will one day be a feast at the end of the ages and it will be a feast that lasts for ever.

> On this mountain, the LORD of hosts will make for all peoples a feast of rich food, a feast of well-aged wines, of rich food filled with marrow, of well-aged wines strained clear. And he will destroy on this mountain the shroud that is cast over all peoples, the sheet that is spread over all nations; he will swallow up death for ever.
>
> *Isaiah 25.6–7*

All of this gives us the background for reading the Gospels, for the miracles where Jesus is the host and feeds the five thousand and the four thousand, for the parables about banquets at the end of the ages and for the institution of the Eucharist, the central act of Christian worship, given to us by the Lord, which draws together so many of these themes.

The Eucharist looks back to the great tradition of meals and sacrifice in the Old Testament and especially to the Passover meal. The Eucharist is the meal at which God himself is our host and welcomes us to sit at table and eat. The Eucharist is the meal at which Jesus himself is our spiritual food and drink, our choice portion and our cup. In the words of institution we say: 'The Body of Christ given for you. The Blood of Christ shed for you.' The Eucharist looks forward to the great heavenly banquet when all peoples will be brought together in Christ at the end of the ages.

How is being welcomed an image of being transformed and changed throughout our lives? Each of these great images, as we have seen, is more than a once and for all event. When we first turn to Christ and declare our allegiance to him we are indeed welcomed, just as the Father welcomes back the younger son in the story in Luke 15. This is the first miracle of the Christian life. But the second is that we go on being welcomed back to the table. God continues to extend his patience and love to us month by month, year by year. We will be welcomed at God's table in heaven, with all of God's people, not because we are good, not because we achieved great things for God but because of God's own grace and love. As it was in the beginning so it will be for ever.

It is God's grace, summed up in this picture, which is so transforming year after year after year through all of life's changing scenes. I do not need to fight for my place in the world. God is my portion and my inheritance. I do not need to fight to be able to survive. God welcomes me into this life and into eternal life. At each great crisis of my life and in the months in between, I am challenged to come back to this great unshakeable truth: God welcomes me; God welcomes you; God welcomes all of us.

The battle for Christian maturity is a battle, as we have seen, between fear and anxiety and is caught so well in these psalms of trust and assurance. Will we have the confidence to understand and believe that we are created because we are loved and to live from that centre of love? Or will our lives be shaped by the anxiety that perhaps there has been some mistake and we have no permanent place in God's purpose?

Many Christians down the years have found immense comfort in George Herbert's poem, 'Love', which draws together so many of these themes. If you know it well, you will not mind returning to it again. If you do not know it, then take time to read it over and absorb its many meanings in the light of this beautiful image of God as host welcoming us to the table:

> Love bade me welcome: yet my soul drew back,
>> Guilty of dust and sin.
> But quick-eyed love, observing me grow slack
>> From my first entrance in,
> Drew nearer to me, sweetly questioning,
>> If I lacked anything.
> A guest, I answered, worthy to be here:
>> Love said: you shall be he.
> I the unkind, ungrateful? Ah, my dear,
>> I cannot look on thee.
> Love took my hand and smiling did reply,
>> Who made the eyes but I?
> Truth, Lord, but I have marred them: let my shame
>> Go where it doth deserve.
> And know you not, says Love, who bore the blame?
>> My dear, then I will serve.
> You must sit down, says Love, and taste my meat:
>> So I did sit and eat.

George Herbert

Sharing your story

What is the most important meal in the life of your family in the course of the year? It may be a regular meal each week – or a meal at a special time of year. Who is the host and who are the guests? What are the different traditions?

Tell one another the story of your engagement with the Eucharist through your life. How much has this meant to you? How far has your understanding changed over time? What is the most important part of the service?

You may want to share as a whole group; or one person might prepare in advance and tell part of their story; or you might want to share in twos or threes.

If you are reading this book on your own then take some time at this point to journal and look back on the way this sense of being welcomed has surfaced in your life.

A film or song clip

See page 80 for suggestions.

Part 2 Experiencing God's love through the Gospel of John

A testimony

Two of the group should read the story aloud, each speaking alternate lines.

> We've told that story thousands of time.
>
> *But we never mind telling it again.*
>
> Picture the shore of Galilee in the evening.
>
> *We'd been hanging about all day hoping to see Jesus again. Nothing was happening.*
>
> Peter wanted to go fishing. The pull of the old life was strong.
>
> *We got two of the boats out and pulled out into the lake.*
>
> We worked all night. Throwing the nets out. Hauling them in again.
>
> *Each time – nothing.*

I'd only known that happen once before. We all knew the lake.

Not one fish. We were exhausted. Hungry and thirsty at the end of the night.

Just before daybreak we saw the light of a fire a little way back from the beach.

Who could be there at this time of day? We steered towards it.

There was a man on the shore. We saw him as the sun came up.

He called out to us: 'Children, you have no fish.'

It wasn't a question. How did he know that?

And why was he calling us children?

We said, 'No', in any case.

Then he said: 'Cast your net to the right side of the boat and you will find some.'

We'd heard that before, a long time ago, the other time we caught nothing.

We cast the nets straight away. The other boat was way behind us.

Immediately the fish swam straight into the net. The biggest catch I'd ever seen.

We couldn't lift it into the boat. We looked back to the shore.

The stranger was still there.

Someone said what we were all thinking: 'It is the Lord.'

Peter wasn't thinking straight. He put some clothes on and jumped into the sea.

The rest of us stayed with the fish. The other boat came and helped us back to land.

Then we saw the fire we had first seen in the darkness before dawn. We stood round it warming ourselves.

There were fish cooking already and flat loaves of bread.

'Bring some of the fish you've caught,' said Jesus.

Peter went on board. He was somehow filled with strength now. On his own he hauled the net ashore.

We counted them later in amazement, 153 fish. No tears in the net.

When Peter came back with the fish we laid them on the fire.

Jesus had set logs out in a circle. He asked us to sit down. I'll never forget that invitation.

'Come and have breakfast.' We knew it was him now.

He took the bread and gave it to us one by one. He did the same with the fish.

We were his guests. This was his table.

Just as it was when we travelled with him.

Just as it is now when we meet together.

Just as it will be at the great banquet.

Now come and eat!

Retold from John 21.1–13

Jesus said: 'I am the bread of life. Whoever comes to me will never be hungry and whoever believes in me will never be thirsty.'

John 6.35

Sharing together

One of the group should say a short grace before you serve the meal that has been prepared.

As you eat and drink together remember the words of Psalm 16: The Lord is my portion and my cup.

What does it mean to you that God welcomes you to his table now and in the future?

Look back over the five images we have explored through this course. To be a Christian means to be:

- Rooted
- Washed
- Enlightened
- Tended
- Welcomed

... through the whole of our lives.

Which is your favourite of the five images and why?

What will you be taking with you from these five sessions?

Part 3 Experiencing God's love through habits and practices

One of the habits arising from this section is clearly the habit and discipline of sharing in the Eucharist. It would be good to talk through not only the frequency you share in the Eucharist but also the ways in which it is helpful to remember that Holy Communion is a meal at which God is our host and which we share with other pilgrims in the way.

One habit that has declined among Christians in the United Kingdom is the very simple habit of saying grace at meals, whether we eat them on our own or with others. Ask one another about your experience of saying grace and encourage one another to introduce that habit on at least some occasions in the week.

The third habit that springs from this theme of being welcomed is, of course, hospitality, which has always been seen as a deeply Christian virtue and is commended in the New Testament. Hospitality builds strong bonds of friendship between Christians. It can also be a really helpful way of extending Christian love to those outside the Church community.

However, many of us also find hospitality quite difficult. As we invite other people into our homes we are revealing more of ourselves to them. Perhaps our house will not be as grand as their house. Perhaps the children will misbehave dreadfully. Perhaps the cooking will not be up to very much. Perhaps we will be judged and found wanting.

The way through these fears is, I think, to focus on the image at the heart of this session. God welcomes us to the table, just as we are. In that way we are to welcome other people, offering what we can in Christian love.

What is the pattern and habit of Christian hospitality you have developed over the years? How will you try and change it over this next year?

For discussion

- Which of these habits and practices will you pay attention to in the coming year?

- What new insights about God's love are you taking away from this session?

Prayers together

Before you pray, clear away the dishes or move to a different part of the house. Spend a few moments in quietness and rest remembering that you are welcomed into God's presence.

Guard me, O God, for I have put my trust in you
I say to you, O LORD: You are my LORD
I have no good apart from you

I say to the holy ones who are in the land
And to their leaders: All my delight is in them

Those who choose another God multiply their sorrows
I will not pour out their offerings of blood
I will not speak their name with my lips

The LORD is my choice portion and my cup
You continue to be my lot

The boundary lines have fallen for me in good places
There is a good inheritance for me

I bless the LORD who counsels me
In the night also he instructs my heart

I keep the LORD before me always
Because he is at my right hand I shall not be moved

Therefore my heart rejoices and my inner being shouts for joy
My flesh also rests secure

For you have not forsaken my soul to Sheol
You have not allowed your holy one to see destruction

You show me the path of life. Fullness of joy is in your presence
Pleasures for evermore are at your right hand.

Psalm 16

A time of open prayer or one person may lead prepared intercessions.

Pray for one another and for any questions that have arisen.

Pray for one another in your intention to enter more deeply into the Eucharist; to introduce grace at meals; to practise hospitality.

End with the Lord's Prayer introduced by:

Trusting in the compassion of God,
As our Saviour taught us so we pray:
Our Father in heaven ...

Now, LORD, you let your servant go in peace;
Your word has been fulfilled.

My own eyes have seen the salvation
Which you have prepared in the sight of every people.

A light to reveal you to the nations
And the glory of your people Israel.

Glory to the Father and to the Son
And to the Holy Spirit
As it was in the beginning, is now
And shall be for ever. Amen.

The Song of Simeon

Bless the LORD, O my soul,
And all that is within me bless his holy name

Bless the LORD, O my soul,
And forget not all his benefits

Who forgives all your sins
And heals all your infirmities

Who redeems your life from the Pit
And crowns you with faithful love and compassion

Who satisfies you with good things
So that your youth is renewed like an eagle's.

Psalm 103.1–5

For reflection and practice by group members after the session

- Write down the steps you need to take to build the good habits you explored in the session.

- Take one practical step in this direction.